THE LIFE AND TIMES
OF BERT MORGAN

Florence Amelia Morgan

MINERVA PRESS
MONTREUX LONDON WASHINGTON

First Published 1996 by
MINERVA PRESS
195 Knightsbridge
London SW7 1RE

Printed in Great Britain by
B.W.D. Ltd., Northolt, Middlesex

THE LIFE AND TIMES
OF BERT MORGAN

Florence Amelia Bozza

Bert Alfred Morgan

My dear husband Bert Alfred Morgan died on September 12th, 1987 aged eighty-seven and I was seventy-six at the time.

I am now eighty-three and have put on to paper my memories of our lives together.

Bert fought in two World Wars as an Able Seaman.

Bert Alfred Morgan was fired with enthusiasm. His brother Bill was in France fighting for his country so he felt the need to do his bit also.

Although only sixteen and a half in the year 1916, throwing caution to the winds, he went to join the Royal Navy. Bert never had any doubts about what he wanted to do, so took himself off to the recruiting office in Stratford, London and joined up. His dad, Bill Morgan, said, "You'll be sorry, my lad."

Bert's first encounter with the Navy was to be sent to a training ship in Portsmouth which turned out to be a large wooden sailing ship that was stationed there. He wasn't there long before he began to realize his father might have been right. The training was hard and rigorous, still with the 'Nelson touch', according to Bert in later years. I remember him mentioning briefly it could not have been worse for them all had they been criminals. I know one of the hardships was to go barefoot, whatever the weather, except Sundays when they were allowed to wear their boots. Every morning they had to go up and over the rigging, and the last one down got the stonecky (a type of whip) which was cruel as there's always a last one, but the boys became men and were honed to survival.

When they were paid their sixpence at the end of the week, tuppence was stopped for a stamp and card to write home. Bert and some others used to run all the way to a village where a lady used to let them have a slice of bread and jam for a penny each.

Writing home was strictly supervised so they could not write what they wanted.

With his training finished Bert proudly joined his first ship at Dover, the *H M S Glatton*. Although I would only have been six years old at the time, I know he must have cut a dashing sight in his sailor's uniform along with all the others, this little cockney sparrow, now prepared for war (courtesy of the 'Nelson touch').

The *Glatton* was being prepared to leave so when they had coaled ship – they used coal in those days – she was ready to sail. As irony would have it Bert had been at sea for about an hour when a bomb went off inside the *Glatton* and he found himself in the sea swimming for his life. Later he learned that it was thought an enemy agent had placed the bomb in with the coal. The survivors were picked up quite quickly, but it was a day or so before they were put ashore, so he was posted missing. By the time he was kitted out and sent home, his family thought he was dead. Thus, his first experience of truly being an Able Seaman.

When Bert was on naval leave he used to pop in and see my brothers who were always pleased to see him. I can remember my sister Rose and I, (Flo), being sent out of the room while they gave him something called Chinese torture; there was always a lot of laughing and fooling around. They would pick him up and put him on the table, then you could hear shouts for mercy amid more laughter coming from the parlour in my parent's greengrocer's shop. I personally think they had an unfair advantage of him, as I had four brothers: Frank, Henry, Richard and Albert, all of good stature, and Bert was only five foot four.

When their pow-wow was over, about the usual rigmarole men talk about – football, cricket, boxing and the like – Bert would eventually leave and come outside where Rose and I would be playing hopscotch with our friends. We would jump up and touch his dicky for luck (his dicky being, I hasten to add, his sailor collar).

Bert was a good natured guy: he never seemed to mind our hands, all covered in chalk, from hopscotch; he used to ruffle our hair and then was on his way.

Bert lived a few houses down from our shop in Campbell Road, on the opposite side of the street, with his mother, Caroline, his dad, Bill, his older brother, Bill, and his three sisters, Dorothy, Violet and Ivy. Their house was just before the Lord Campbell, a public house, which was just past their house, on a corner.

When Bert was thirteen years old, he used to get up at five o'clock in the morning to do the milk round for these people who had a dairy. They were Welsh and it was hard work, but he did it to help his mum, who did outdoor work making little boys' trousers on the machine as times were hard.

One of Bert's most precious possessions was a beautiful Bible that was presented to him for his excellence in Biblical knowledge when he was fourteen years of age, at Knapp Road School.

He also won a scholarship for Chemistry, and went to St. Thomas School, Bow Common Lane. He was there about a year, and left because his parents could not afford the books he needed.

He then got a job as a messenger boy. His job was to walk people's dogs in the park, and also run messages. His uniform was navy blue, with a red pillbox hat.

Bert still needed to get a better job, so he left the messengers and went back to the Welsh dairy, and stayed there until the time he joined the Navy. It was when he told my brother Frank that Frank said,
"Well, don't forgot to write. We will keep in touch."

Bert said he would, and they did.

According to my brothers, Bert was still in the Baltic on Russian convoy. It was years later that I learnt what Bert really felt for the Russians: he said the poor devils fought so hard, and the powers-that-be in this country at that time could have done much more to help them but they were dragging their feet; they wanted food and help; and this was 1919. The enemy had driven the Russians right back to the Russian Steppes, a monumental landmark; pushed beyond human endurance, with no food, very few weapons, and executing the scorched earth policy of setting fire to everything as they went, so the oncoming enemy had nothing. This worked, but in the end they also were starving. Maybe that is what worried Bert. He thought we should have done much more for our Allies. The weather was freezing, the sailors had to take turns chipping the ice off the rails, and if they didn't keep moving they felt as if they would freeze to the deck. You could understand how hard it must have been for the Russians.

The sea froze around them, as they sailed through the ice floes. Bert said that the collar of his coat was frozen and his chin was all chafed and sore: it was a race against the elements.

He was either on the *Cambrain* or the *Verity*, I cannot be sure, but the severity of the weather was the same for all of them.

In Italy, my mum's dad, Ronald Amato, shared some chestnut trees and olive trees with his brother, but as he was going back and forth to England, he gave his share of the trees to his brother.

Grandad and Grandma Amato used to journey to England every year bringing their children with them.

I said to Mum, how on earth did you manage? Well, my mother used to stay behind until her babies were born, and then followed on about three weeks later. I said it could not have been easy. Mum said it wasn't but they managed. Mum said that she was only three weeks old when she was brought to England and the last to come was Elizabeth, she was the baby. Mum said there were seven of us children, we sadly lost a boy. He was in his teens and his name was Joe. When Mother spoke of her brother she had a far away look in her eyes.

I asked Mum to tell me about her home in Italy. So Mother told me that they lived on the side of a mountain in a place called Massa Lubrense, where they had a lovely view across the sea to the island of Capri. When she was about twelve, she used to have to go and fetch the milk. They did not have milkmen leaving it on the doorstep like they do in this country. She would put her wooden shoes on and say,
"These shoes hurt my heels, Mum," and her mum said:
"Well, do what I used to do, and go into the Church, and put some candle grease on them. So Mum would set off swinging the milk can that she carried with her. Halfway down, she would come to a little door in the mountainside, open the door and go inside. It was a lovely little church, with its cool dark interior. Mum would light a candle and pour some grease into the cuts in her heels, and this would help a lot, then she would hurry down to catch the ferry to Capri.

Capri was a lush island covered in grasses, with lots of cows grazing there. Mother said there was a big house on Capri that fascinated her; it had lots of steps, and goldfish pools on the sides of them. Mother said it was a most beautiful place.

I wanted to know who the big house belonged to on Capri. Mum said:

"Oh, some rich people I suppose. Questions, questions!"
Mum would say:
"Away with you girl, I am busy!" but secretly I think Mum liked
to talk about her homeland.

Today people tell me I am the living image of my mother. My
grandfather, Mum's dad, Ronald Amato, was tall with a moustache
that hung down at the sides. He always dressed smartly, and wore his
gold watch and chain. Today he would probably be mugged for it; as
I remember, the chain was a very thick one. My grandma Amato was
short and stout, and had lovely blue-black hair pulled back off her
face, and done in a bun at the back of her head. My sister Rose had
blue-black hair when she was young, and resembled my grandmother,
and wasn't a bad looker. A large photo used to hang in the shop
parlour of the grandparents'. I once asked why Grandad was sitting
and Grandma was standing, and was told that Grandfather would
tower over her, as he was tall. (I suppose I should have worked that
out for myself.) I can almost hear Grandad Amato talking about his
beloved Italy. He used to mention Amalfi and Genoa. I am sure he
was homesick. I wish I had been more attentive when he spoke to me
of Naples and other such places; he always wanted talk about his
homeland, he said it was lovely.

When Grandad first came to England, another man, who also used
to make ice cream, came also; his name was Rossi. They came to
make their fortune, and travelled with Grandad and his family, and I
think Rossi did make it to the big time, but my grandad used to like a
game of cards, so it was a sort of hit and miss existence. I know he
had lots of friends and was a likeable old chap.

When Grandad's papers came through that made him naturalized
and meant he could stay in this country for good and not have to go
back every six months, which meant that he could make ice cream all
the year round if he liked, the family was very happy to settle down
for good and make England their home. Meanwhile back in Italy,
Alfonso Bozza, who was later to be my Dad, was nearly nineteen, and
was loading lemons on to a British ship. He was always asking the
Captain to take him to England. One day the Captain agreed to let
him work his passage. When they reached the London Docks, he was

told where Poplar was and that he would join some other Italians there.

This Alfonso Bozza did, and managed to get himself a job in a fruiterers with some other Neapolitans, people of his own kind, which was just as well because he could not speak English.

When my Mum met Alfonso Bozza, she proceeded to try and teach him English, and they kept company for about a year. Mum, who was Mary Louise Amato, found it hard going, because Alfonso was living with other Italians who were all speaking their own language.

When my parents, Mary and Alfonso, were twenty years old they decided to get married. I have a photo of them in their wedding finery: Dad in his best suit, bowler hat, silver topped cane, cigar, buttonhole, and Dad wore a moustache that is still fashionable today.

Mother wore a beautifully tailored grey silk dress, its tiny waist edged with embroidery; this embroidery was also on the front of the bodice and on the collar. Her lovely hat was piled high with flowers – they made a handsome couple.

Mum asked her friend Annie Barnes to write to Italy for her and Dad, to tell their relatives all about the wedding. Mum's friend Annie was a very clever woman, and well-known in the suffragette movement. She was of very small stature. Mum told me about the time that Annie went up in the tower and scattered leaflets out of the windows. They blew all over the place from that height, and when the police came to catch the culprit, they never bothered with this person who looked like a little girl. Mum said that Annie used to get away with a lot.

My parents, Mary and Alfonso Bozza, started their married life in a little shop in Devast street which was a fruit and greengrocer's. I think that area is Bromley by Bow; they lived there for a few years and then moved to a shop in Campbell Road, Bow. By this time Mother had two children: the eldest, christened Francis, Ricardo, the second child who we called Richard, and then in this house came Henry, her third boy.

Dad said he would like a bigger shop, the shop was small, but he liked Campbell Road, so when a shop became vacant across the road he took it. It was next door to an undertakers, named Adams. Mother said that they were content with this house, it had three bedrooms, and the shop was bigger.

I can see our greengrocer's in my mind's eye, especially at Christmas time: two bird cages hung from the ceiling, with yellow canaries: they used to sing their little hearts out, and Dad always talked to them. He loved animals. There were two rabbits in the back yard, Beigiunairs, I think you called them, and a couple of chickens. At Christmas time you could hardly move in our yard! Boxes would be stacked all over the place, oranges, nuts, sprouts, potatoes, and Dad made the shop look grand, the fruit all in pyramids, silver paper on the tangerines, chains hanging from the shop ceiling, a real feeling of Christmas excitement. Mum and Dad loved this time of the year. Dad would get up at about four in the morning, hire Barwick's cart and horse (Barwick was our coalman), and go trotting off to Spitalfields market. He would do this about twice a week, going through Bow Road, Whitechapel and Aldgate. I remember Dad working very hard, he would just lie down for an hour in the afternoon when things were a bit quieter. We used to sell ice cream and soft drinks at one time until some Italians moved next door. Their name was Milordini, and Dad passed the ice cream and drinks to them. They were very nice people, always smiling, we liked them and we all got on fine.

I used to like to watch the old gentleman breaking thirty-six eggs into the tub, with the vanilla, and the tub sat in a bed of ice. He would swirl the tub around until it was just right; I do not know if it is made like this today, but it was delicious.

Dad's customers loved him. They used to call him Italian Jack. He always gave children tasters. He cut away the bruised fruit and gave it to the children who accompanied their Mums with a cheery word in broken English.

He would rock his head from side to side, and sing his favourite song, 'Veniculi, Venicula'.

Mother had another little boy in this house, and called him Albert. Mum told me that he was her most pretty baby of all. He had a round rosy face, brown curly hair and deep set brown eyes, and lovely skin, although she often said, "All these boys!" and longed for a girl.

Well, two years after Albert, Mother got her wish: she had me, and two years after me, she had Rose. There were two years between each of us: Mother must have had a mating month.

This was very handy on birthdays as one party would do the lot of us.

We all went to Holy Name School, Bow Common Lane. As the time came to go, I remember my brother, Richie, was to collect me and see me home but he could not find me anywhere. A very worried brother came home to find I had come home by myself, not to be thought of today.

When Rose started school, my eldest brother Frank was working as a Singer's sewing machine mechanic, and Richie was starting at the Hotel Cecil, in the West End of London, which was pulled down years ago. The tales he used to come home and tell us! Today, the cat fell in the soup, and rats as big as cats would run up his legs! I didn't believe half of what he told us although my sister and I were young and gullible. He left there to work in a fish shop called Nymans, in Campbell Road. It was a few doors down from us and was well-known for its fish and chips - people used to come from near and far to buy some.

Back at school all our headmistresses were nuns. I remember little Sister Catherine, in her navy blue habit and her white winged headdress. She was so tiny, she used to go around trying to squeeze coppers out of people. She would come into our shop once a week and was given a sixpence. Her tiny hand would stow it away in the pocket of her habit; she would then travel on to St Andrew's Hospital to visit the sick.

The nuns needed every penny they could get. They tried to buy footwear, there were so many children that were barefoot and never knew what it was like to have shoes on their feet. The nuns were always trying to get footwear for them, but when they did manage some, the said boots or shoes nearly always ended up in the pawn shop.

I expect their mothers meant to get them out again, but they were so terribly poor. Even my shoes used to get very run down and split down the backs where they were getting too small before I got new ones, and we were in business. It was hard to believe we were the richest country in the world, at that time.

The drill slips and slippers belonged to the school, for the use of the netball team. Not many girls owned a drill slip, I didn't for one, but I loved netball, and was glad when I was old enough for the first team.

Bert was away at sea, and the war and the time of shortages – when Dad had to dole out what little he could get at market – were over, and letters from Bert were few and far between. I was only interested in what went on at school at that time. One day when we had a match, we donned our drill slips and sashes, and we took it in turns to write on the blackboard, and it was now my turn.

I wrote our school's name in a sort of italics. Our headmistress, Sister Vincent, asked me where I had learnt to do it, and I told her I had learned it from my brother Frank, who wrote what was for sale on the shop window. Sister was impressed, and I felt ten feet tall.

But my state of euphoria did not last very long as I disgraced myself a week later. We were told to stop laughing in class, but I didn't stop quickly enough, so I was sent to the Head.

The thought of being punished by my dear Sister Vincent was punishment enough for me. As the cane came down, it caught in the rosary beads she wore round her waist, with a crucifix on the end. I was about twelve years old. Big black beads went rolling everywhere. I bent down to pick them up.

"Don't touch them," sister said angrily, and that was when I cried. I made up my mind to be very good indeed after that. It was the first and last time I was ever caned.

At this time Richard left the fish shop to work in Angel Lane, Stratford. It was Mother's aunt's shop, who was named Atterano – Sweets, Tobacco, Ice Cream and Cakes.

And what lovely ice cream – the real stuff! I used to love going to see Aunt Atterano. It entailed catching a tram from Bow Road to Stratford, then going down Angel Lane to the shop. Aunt used to give me some chocolates and ice cream, which I loved. Aunt also gave me a shilling which I shared with Rose, my sister.

I smile to myself now when I think of Aunt Atterano being given a lift on Bert's motor bike (a Triumph). He said to her, "You've no need to walk right down Campbell Road and catch a bus – if you're game to sit on my pillion."

About this time, my brothers were getting letters from Bert, their sailor friend. He was stationed in China, then Hong Kong, and was to be there for another two and a half years. I was at school during this time, and was picked for the netball team. The boys used to shout: "Come on azzob..." and I realized this was my name backwards.

Back at Holy Name School, my dear teacher Sister Vincent was encouraging me to take up art and putting plenty of homework my way. I think this was because I did a drawing of the Prince of Wales (Prince Teddy) who was on a World Tour – his head through a newspaper and all the names of the places he'd been – around him. I cannot describe my embarrassment at having to take it all round the school to show to every class. This was enough to put me off art.

A careless comment from a neighbour finally dissuaded me. "You'll never get a scholarship, your father's a foreigner, you're wasting your time." I can see Sister Vincent's face now when I told her.

Around this time Mum asked me if I would take Dad to see Aunt Atterano. He didn't get out much these days. We started our journey up Campbell Road to catch the tram, but we only got as far as Campbell Road bridge and Dad could not go any further. He was having trouble getting his breath and coughing a lot. We had a little rest then we turned back. Mum said Dad's bronchitis and asthma was getting worse, but to him she said, "Never mind, another day perhaps." I said yes, that Aunt Atterano would like that, when he was feeling better.

Dad became very ill, and one cold day in January 1925 he died. I was thirteen and a half and bereft.

It was a great shame as Mother had been planning to get Dad back to Italy for a holiday, thinking it would do him good, but it was too late. He was forty-nine. Any age is a bad time to lose someone in your family.

My sister Rose and I took it badly. As fate would have it a dressmaking friend of Mother's had just made the two of us lovely coats, fawn with a roll collar, and they did up with a large fancy button. Rose and I felt very made up in them when we tried them on, but before we could wear them, they had to be dyed black and the lovely button taken off. After that, I disliked the coat.

I think it was this aunt who first instilled in me the art and love of dressmaking and in later life I became a competent dressmaker.

There were literally crowds of people at Dad's funeral. From upstairs I could see them through a gap in the curtains. I remember how awful I felt that day. How could we lose such a lovely man, the happy-go-lucky Italian Jack that everybody knew and loved? I knew my silent tears were dropping onto my newly dyed coat but I didn't care and I wanted all the people to go away. Above all I wanted my father back with us, to hear him calling in his lyrical voice. I knew he lay just a few yards away in the horse-drawn hearse standing at the curb.

I realize now what a wonderful send-off Dad's funeral was. Hundreds of people walked along with the cortège.

When it was time to go downstairs I could see lots of people pressed up against the window of the shop and, as clearly and as loudly as it could, one of Dad's canaries started singing. I walked with my sister and four brothers into the street. I couldn't help looking at the four gleaming black horses, stately, with their long black plumes of feathers on their heads, and four men dressed in black at their sides. I remember mostly the men's tall black hats they wore, draped with black chiffon that floated out behind their heads as they walked, fixed to the brims and blowing in the wind even though they walked slowly...

I saw many people shedding a tear. Dad had truly been a well-loved somebody – he had showered love on us and on those whom he came in contact with and it had been an honour to know him.

As Aunt Atterano had said, "The world is going to be a sadder place without Alphonso Bozza, our dear Italian Jack" – who cut out the specs from the shop and would give them to the kids with no shoes, his generous weighing to the old neighbours, and his hand full of peanuts to shell for the friends that called for my brothers. And my mother Mary Louise who had met and married her fellow kinsman, she would sing with him no more. A sad loss indeed.

Soon I would be leaving school. Henry and Albert had already left; Frank took over the shop with Henry helping when he could.

Frank was now courting a girl in our own road, called Helen. We called her Nell because she wanted us to, and they were planning to marry in the near future.

My brother's girlfriend Nell was good fun. When we were younger she would put us to bed for Mum, and would always make us laugh, with things like pretending to cut up the bolster and asking how many pounds of sausages do you require Madam, and such like. Yes, we approved of Frank's choice. When I actually left school, I went to stay with Auntie Mac the dressmaker, to get an idea of the trade. It was then I realized how good she was; and when I came home from Finchley I was determined to be a machinist.

When Dad was alive he liked our hair long, but after a couple of months out to work I still looked like a schoolgirl, so I had it cut off. Mother came with me after a job, we went to a firm called Fosters in the Bow Road, and the job was as a machinist, Alfred Street, Bow.

I showed Mrs Foster my school leaving certificate, which said: "Florrie is good at art and needlework, and should do well if given the opportunity."

I thought it was a magic passport to work, but it did not make the desired impression, so I promptly lost faith in it, although I have it still.

Mrs Foster looked at my eyes and said to Mum, "She doesn't want to spoil her eyes at this sort of work."

I was very disappointed. I said to Mum, why couldn't she just say she didn't want anyone? Mum said, "Don't worry, you will get a job all right!" But jobs were not all that easy to come by at that time.

I finally got a job at hat making. It was in Cheapside, a long way for very little money.

After a while this place closed down, so the boss sent me to his sister's firm in Commercial Road. This is where I really learnt the trade, and soon found myself making hats for the neighbours. You know how it is, when people know you can do something, they want one, so I made tricorns with feathers at the side, and the fashionable poe hats, and drew flowers with a hot wire on felt hats. It was all very interesting, but I still hankered after dressmaking.

Although I liked the work, my first love was still to be a dressmaker, so I thought I would give it another try at Fosters in Bow Road as it was near to where I lived in Campbell Road, and I was fed up with travelling to the City. This time I was either lucky or persistent, because I was taken on. Mrs Foster said providing I started on beading first, she would put me on the machine later, so for a couple of months I did beading. It was very interesting, sewing little bugle beads and seed pearls on dresses. I liked doing this, I wanted to learn everything about the job.

True to my boss's word I went on the machine.

I took to it like a duck to water, I suppose because I wanted to so much. Very soon I went piecework, making dresses and skirts and the like, soon to have saved enough for my very own machine.

My brother Frank helped me choose it, and in my brother I had my very own Singer's mechanic, who always used to oil and clean it for me.

Frank mentioned that Bert the sailor would be home from China soon. I said I expected he would be glad to be back.

It was around that time that Frank and Nell were going to tie the knot, so I was able to help Nell, and I made mine and my sister's bridesmaid's dresses; they were pale lavender in colour. A local dressmaker made Nell's wedding dress and Nell's sister Nancy's chief bridesmaid dress. Nell looked lovely in white satin.

Saturday mornings were like a ritual in our house: first, help with the housework, then down to the baths in Violet Road for tuppence a bath, then across the road to the hairdresser to have my hair curled with the curling tongs.

I knew one or two boys my own age. Being asked to the pictures meant seeing them inside: pay for yourself. Well, I suppose they never earnt much; if they bought sweets, you could count yourself lucky to get a couple.

While I was working at Fosters as a machinist, Bert's sister Ivy asked me if I could get her a job at the place where I worked. She said she would love to be a machinist. She was working in a bakers, and wasn't very happy there and said she was going nowhere.

So I promised I would ask for her. I explained that I had first to work on beading, and she said she would not mind doing that.

So I asked my boss about her, and my boss said that if I would take her under my wing and teach her the trade, I could take her on.

When I told Ivy she was very pleased. "When do I start?" she asked. I said, "Right away if you like."

Well, Ivy turned out to be a very good dressmaker and was soon earning a good wage.

A few years later I made her wedding dress, and with my sister-in-law's help (that was Vera), we beaded the Elizabethan collar and beaded the train, with diamanté stones, seed pearls and bugle beads. It was really lovely – she said she felt like a queen, and we said she looked like one.

At this time I was getting on for sixteen. Bert came to see us as usual, and remarked on how we girls had grown. I suppose I was a bit of a surprise, I had grown from a schoolgirl into a young flapper: that's what teenagers were known as in those days.

As Bert was stationed in Chatham we saw a lot of him, and as his friends had either got married or moved away, he had lost touch, having been away so long.

I had been on piecework for some time now and was earning what was considered a man's money, around two pounds ten shillings a week. It sounds funny now but that's how it was then, in 1927 or thereabouts.

Bert said he would like to get some letters, and would my mother mind if I wrote to him, to keep him in the picture?

As I was nearing sixteen, and Bert was twenty seven, I daresay the difference in our ages was a bit hard to take.

Mother said to him, "If you don't mind me reading them too." Bert looked at me, I shrugged and said, "All right by me", so we started to correspond.

Next time Bert was home, he asked mother if he could take me to the pictures. Mum said, "No harm in that I suppose", so we decided to go to the Bow Palace in Bow Road.

Bert gave me the money for some sweets; I bought a quarter of liquorice allsorts for four pence.

I always remember everything about my first date with Bert, holding his arm and being treated with courtesy, I felt very grown up, which I hadn't felt before.

February the fourteenth was drawing near. I got together with two of my friends, Dorothy and Lilly, we were all about the same age, nearing sixteen. Our talk was all about Valentine cards, how many to buy, and to make sure we wouldn't be sending them to the same boys. We did a lot of laughing when choosing them – the same things still go on today – and, having decided, we were ready to despatch them to our chosen Valentines. For a bit of fun I sent one to Bert Morgan because actually, I didn't think anyone else would.

Well, time went on, I had forgotten all about Valentines. I suppose it was about six weeks after when Bert came to see us again. He was on weekend furlow, I think he called it.

Mum went out of the room to make a cup of tea, when Bert handed me a bunch of ribbons. I recognised them at once, they had been taken off the Valentine card I had sent him. He said, "I think these are yours". I burst out laughing and took them off him. He said, "Do you remember the rhyme that went with them?" "Of course I do," I said. It went,
"If to me you would be true, please return this piece of blue.
If with me you would be seen please return this piece of green.
If to me you will be wed, please return this piece of red."

"Oh," said Bert, "It was you then! I caught you out then!

I said, "I should have feigned ignorance, but you took me by surprise, after all this time."

Mum came in with the tea, and asked what was all the laughing about. We told her, and she joined in the joke. At that time it was just a girlish prank, I had no thoughts of ever marrying Bert or anyone else at that time, but I suppose some sort of line had been crossed without us realizing it.

My brother Frank came in and they chatted for a while. As Frank went, he said to Bert, "You should be taking some nice young girl out."
Bert said, "Bring me one then, and I will."

When Bert went, he said he was going to see his cousin Arthur, and if we didn't see him before, we would see him on his next leave.

I went to the pictures with two girl friends, to a place called Buzzes. Today it would be called a dump, but we enjoyed it. There was a lady playing a piano fast and loud for cowboys and Indians, slow and dreamy for love scenes: she was very good. She could make that piano sound like thunder and lightning, or practically anything that the film called for. Happy days.

We were easily pleased in those days. The picture palace was situated under the railway arches, so every now and again there was the sound of trains overhead.

The noisy giant steam trains of the Old Great Western Railway rumbled on their way to the West Country, Devon and Cornwall.

Funny to think of that now, as I live in Devon.

By now Rose was leaving school, and went to work for Bryant & Mays, the match people. She seemed quite happy there, joining later in the netball team. I can picture her now: creamy skin, blue-black hair. We used to call her Pola Negri (a film star of my time), no less.

We had an unkind neighbour who used to comment to Mother things like, "He's old enough to be her father" (referring to Bert).

Well if there was one thing destined to throw us together, it was remarks like that, so when I was seventeen and Bert bought me a dress ring, I flashed it around, saying nothing for the benefit of the busybodies.

Bert eventually finished his twelve years in the Navy, and suddenly found himself out of work. He thought about signing on again but had already lost a girlfriend who wouldn't wait for him, so decided against it, just signing for naval reserve, to be called on if his country needed him.

After trying for several jobs with no luck, he wrote to the Sailors and Soldiers Association. They sent back a card telling him to go to Romford, to clean telephone boxes, and that he was the only one put forward for the job. Unfortunately the distance involved made this impossible (four buses a day) and the princely sum of forty-two shillings a week. I still have the card. Fortunately, Bert's brother Bill got him a painting job, painting school railings and the like. It was then he bought the second-hand motor bike (the very same that dear Aunt Atterano braved a pillion ride on).

One evening we were off to the Stratford Broadway Pictures, and were walking up Devon's road, on our way to catch the bus in Bow Road to take us there, when Bert said, "Why are you looking sad?"
I said, "I didn't realize, I was thinking about my Dad, and that you will never know him."
"But I did know him."
"Did you, Bert?" I said.
"Yes, I often spoke to him. You must have been at school."
"Oh, I am pleased."

It was lovely to know that Bert had known him and often spoke to him.
"Your Dad always said hello, and asked where I was off to. Once when I was going swimming, your Dad said are you going to the swimming baths, I had a towel under my arm, so yes, I was going

swimming. Another time, when I was dressed in my best, your Dad said are you going to see your little canary, my canary being my current girlfriend. I said yes I am going to see my girlfriend. If your Dad was standing at the door of the shop I always spoke to him."

"Bert, it has made me so happy to think you knew him."

Another thing I remember about my dad, he used to go on these coach outings each year from a public house in Devon's Road, I think it was called The Duke's Head. You went up Devon's Road, over the railway bridge, and down the other side of the bridge, and on the corner was the Duke's Head.

He would go out in his best, his nice trilby, always a cigar in his mouth, and there would be the Charabanc waiting; it was for men only.

A huge crowd of children would gather and would shout, "Throw out your mouldies, throw out your mouldies," and a huge shower of coppers would be showered over the children, pennies, ha'pennies and farthings, and what a scramble there would be. Then the coach would move off to Brighton or wherever. That's how it would be in those far-off days, it was a sort of a custom that they always carried out.

But I know Dad enjoyed it, and he always brought Rose and I a little gift.

Some evenings we spent at home, I would ask Bert about the First World War. He told me he had a shipmate called Len, who was a diver. Len would sometimes visit the family, who made him very welcome, he was very sweet on Bert's sister Dorothy, but unfortunately for Len, her affections were for a chap named Syd, whom Dorothy later married; she became Mrs Sydney Joyce. On asking Bert what divers did, he said that ships carried a large sheet of what looked like plastic rubber, and if the ship was holed in combat they had to fix this material to the deck and take it down the side of the ship, then underneath and up the other side and fix it to the deck. No easy task, but it enabled them to get to port for repairs. I found that very interesting.

I also learnt that all sailors had nicknames, Bert's was Rattler Morgan. I had heard him called Rattler, I used to know a lot of nicknames but have forgotten them now. I daresay that many an old First World War seaman could rattle tham off.

Bert still went to Laindon on the motor bike, on the painting job. The bike served him well, and the job lasted for about a year and a half in all.

He then got himself a job with a firm called Ragusa Ashphalt Company. He was called a potman. The work was very hard, it meant breaking up lumps of ashphalt, putting them in the pot to boil, then going up ladders with boiling buckets of ashphalt. You had to keep the spreader going.

He worked away from home a lot which meant he earned more money, provided there was plenty of work.

When I was eighteen, Bert bought me a row of Ciro pearls in Bond Street, which I treasured; they did not cost that much, as we were saving every penny and not spending on unnecessary things. It took ages to save a couple of pounds in those days.

We started a joint savings book. Bert gave me what he could each week and it began to tot up slowly. His only luxury was Black Cat cigarettes; luckily he wasn't a heavy smoker. He used to save the coupons, and I changed them for a case of cutlery for my bottom drawer. Later I sent for a box Brownie camera, which was a luxury in those days as very few people owned one. We decided it was a must, we could snap friends and their children, and it came in very useful.

We had some friends, called Mary and Alf Knight, who lived in Dagenham. They had a little girl, and we sometimes spent weekends at their house. We also stayed at Bert's brother's house in Laindon, where we spent some nice times with Bill, Nell and the children, and our camera came in useful.

It's very nice to look back at these happy times, when all the children were small.

It was Mary and Alf, of Gale Street, Dagenham's council estate, who said to us one weekend when we were staying there, if you are thinking of getting married, why don't you get your name put down for one of these council houses. Just write to County Hall, tell them you are thinking of getting married and ask was there a chance of getting a house.

We could not believe it would be that easy, but said we would write to them. A couple of weeks later we received a reply. It said they would like a few particulars, which we duly gave them.

We boarded the train to Gale Street Halt, Dagenham – that is what the station was called then, before it was called Becontree. We wanted to let our friends know of our progress. We did not have telephones then, at least the ordinary individual didn't. A week later we received another letter. It said to let them know as soon as we put up our banns, so we had to decide on a date.

We finally decided on March the twenty-eighth, which was Easter time, having thought it would be better for everyone.

That gave us about two months. My Aunt Mac, so called because she had married a Scot, we called her Aunt Lizzie really, always said she would make my wedding dress, so with that settled, I set about making the bridesmaids' dresses, of which there were four.

There were Bert's two sisters, Ivy and Violet, my sister Rose and Nell, who was courting my brother Henry at the time – she was my friend Mary's sister.

Mum gave me some nice things, including a lovely bedspread and some of her old cutlery to use for cooking utensils, she also saved a couple of Christmas puddings, for the dinner.

In those days you didn't make present lists, you were grateful for whatever you received, as money was short. Bert was putting in as many hours as he could, and I was saving steadily.

The wedding day was getting near. I received some nice presents from the place where I worked, from Daddy Harris, as we fondly called him, and the girls, including Mr Harris's daughter Flora; my previous boss Mrs Foster also sent a present.

I made a quick visit to Finchley, to Aunt Mac, for a fitting for my wedding dress. It was beautiful, as I knew it would be. It was made of a soft white satin, and Aunt was doing a lot of hand trimming, called cockle shell, and very pretty it looked, and it being the month of March and still cold, Aunt had made a little scalloped coatee to go with it. I realized how lucky I was.

The bridesmaids also had fittings. Their dresses were a pale flimsy material, lemon colour, with pink tulips all over the pattern: extremely pretty. They had lemon picture hats to go with the dresses.

I am afraid Rose gave me a bit of trouble: she wanted to wear her brim up while the others wore theirs down. I think they compromised by all wearing them half way.

Bert chose a brown suit. He wasn't sure if he liked it or not. We all assured him it was very nice.

There was only the old box camera for photos. We could not afford a photographer, so Bert's dad would be consigned to the camera.

We duly sent the letter to County Hall, telling them we had put the banns up, at Holy Name Church in Bow Common Lane. Keeping our fingers crossed, we waited for a reply. At the end of that first week, the reply came. We were to go to Cannonsleigh Road rents office to collect some keys.

We went post-haste. When we arrived, we were given two sets of keys. Off we went clutching the keys, wondering what we were going to see.

We were to look at two houses in Sheppey Road. If you can imagine what a big building site looks like, heaps of rubble, some small train lines used by the builder, we rounded a corner and there was Sheppey Road. I said to Bert they must be it. There was a row of finished houses, and then some with just the footings in. We made our way to the last two finished ones. Number two hundred and six was the one we tried the key in. We went inside. On the right we opened the door to the living room – today it would be called the lounge. It was a nice size; in one corner it was shaped like an archway, very decorative with a nice square window to the front of the house.

We bore round to the right, and opened the door to the kitchen. A nice square kitchen, a pantry in the corner, and a cupboard facing the back door, this cupboard was in two halves with a top and bottom half, very useful.

We were highly delighted with our nice square kitchen. In the far corner was something we considered very modern, (now it would be considered just an old gas copper boiler). Now I think of it, I seem to recollect it resembled a witch's cauldron – steam as well, only there wasn't a bonfire underneath – you lit it with a match, though. When the water was hot enough, you pumped it upstairs to the bathroom, by a handle on the wall.

Antiquated, but so very efficient, and welcome for those days, as we'd never been used to this much comfort. We were thankful for it.

I couldn't resist having a go at the pump.
"Seems easy enough," I said to Bert.
"Good," was his reply, "that will be your job then." My cheeky little sailor boy.
I said, "Watch it, I haven't married you yet."

Then we dashed upstairs to see what the two bedrooms looked like. The door facing us turned out to be a really big room spanning the width of the house and overlooking the front, with a long narrow window, a fitted cupboard in one corner and an interesting little fireplace at the other end. The other bedroom was much smaller, but also had a cupboard and fireplace. Next – sheer luxury – a bathroom and toilet in one.

This was a step up in the world. We had never owned a bathroom, either of us, neither had anyone else we knew, perhaps with the exception of my Auntie Mac, who lived in Finchley.

The small bedroom and bathroom overlooked the back, so we went back downstairs to take a closer look at the garden. We strolled about the garden hand in hand, then right up to the back fence and watched a steam train go by. It was a thrill. There were no electric trains then.

Looking back now, little did we realize then that in a few short years Bert would be fighting for his country on some foreign shore and I would be running for my life in this very garden with our small child, while enemy planes flew over our house and followed the trains, machine-gunning them. But for now we were quite happy. Although we looked at another house, it had a small hallway. The living room had three doors, into the hallway, kitchen and up the stairs, which opened like a cupboard. But it was the side gate I disliked. I told Bert I would sooner have the porch house that we had first seen.

Bert often worked away, and he now had to go where the work was. Not his fault. He said, "If you're sure." I said I would be nervous when he was away.
He said, "Fair enough."

He told me not to worry and that I would soon make some friends. I thought, I hope so. We took the keys back to the rents office and paid five shillings on the ones for 206 Sheppey Road, Dagenham, and could now keep these. They were ours.

Feeling content with our lot, we made our way back to Campbell Road to tell our respective families all our news.

When I reflect now, it seems amazing that we could see the planes landing and taking off from Fairlop Aerodrome from our bedroom window, and nothing but poppy fields and cornflowers, all growing wild. A lovely sight, we considered we lived in the country. Everything in our eyes was beautiful and we were impatient for it all to happen.

Our families were very pleased about our new abode, and of course they all wanted to have a look, so each time we went there to take our belongings we were collecting for our home, they all took it in turns to come with us.

My brother Henry gamely struggled with an orange mottled kerb surround for the fireplace in the living room. He said it weighed a ton. It was his present to us. He was so proud of it, and we thought it looked the tops, and were to spend many a happy time together, with our feet resting on that surround.

Curtains were the next important item on the agenda, so I took myself off to Green Lane in East Ham to choose some material. After making them on my machine, we hung them on wires (that's how you did it in those days).

A good friend of the family, Mrs Godfrey, gave Bert and I a beautiful tablecloth and six napkins to match.

Mrs Godfrey was the licensee of a public house in Bow, called The Widow's Son, called thus because when her son went off to sea he asked her to save him a hot cross bun. So each year she hung one in a net in the bar. She was a really nice person and very kind. Her son never did come home.

Bert and I studied our Post Office book and did some calculations. There was exactly sixty-five pounds in it.

After deducting money for the marriage licence, drinks and some incidentals, there would be about fifty pounds left.

We decided to go to a place called Crisp Street, a much favoured place for shopping in our area, as it was close at hand. We needed to try and furnish our home on what was left. We finally ended up in a shop called Neals Furniture Store. An eager salesman showed us around. We chose a shiny brown three piece suite, a dining table with Queen Anne legs and four chairs to match, and picked a green carpet that matched the curtains. Although it was what was known as a 'carpet square', it was large and did nearly touch the walls.

Upstairs in the furniture shop we chose the bedroom suite, dressing table, chest of drawers and our very own brand new double bed. We would have to make do with the cupboards already there.

Looking back it doesn't seem feasible, we had bought so much for so little. I remember the three piece costing fifteen pounds but cannot recall the exact prices of the other things, except that everything was paid for, including blankets and pillows. Sheets, I had in my bottom drawer, along with some other linen I had bought along the way. We found we had enough left for some lino, and they kindly made us a present of a mat for our custom. Having arranged to have it delivered on Saturday morning, from the amount of help we were promised it sounded like all hands on deck. I considered myself very fortunate indeed: not many couples had a start like ours.

That weekend the lino was laid in the bedroom, the bed set up, dressing table and chest of drawers in their places. Downstairs, we enjoyed pushing the furniture around, trying it out in different places, until we were satisfied. We ended up doing it the age old way, arm chair each side of the fireplace, table in the middle, chairs round the table settee under the window, ornaments on the mantelpiece: it all sounds very ordinary, but it wasn't to us, our very first lovely home.

Among our wedding gifts, there was another mat and a mirror which completed the downstairs room. My friend and I went up to make the bed, and put the rest of the linen in the drawers. I knew there were still a lot of things I needed, and it would take a lot of time to get them, but for now Bert and I were content.

Our friends in Gale Street had made us a kitchen table as a present, and my mother had given us two wooden chairs for which I was very glad. I rushed around for a last minute dust, then gave the letterbox a good polish; it was a brass one, and looked very smart. All was now ready to move in to after the wedding.

We locked the door, had a last look up at the windows then made our way to the station, and the next part of our preparations.

The twenty-eighth of March was Easter that year. At Easter the Church is in mourning, and all the statues are draped in purple cloth, so we were not very popular with Father Reardon.

We did not choose Easter on purpose, it was just the way things turned out. Also I was marrying a Protestant.

Father Reardon had a few talks with Bert. He wanted to know if we should have any children, would he let them become Catholics? Bert told him that it would be entirely up to me should we be lucky enough. I assured the priest that they would be Catholic.

We cleared the bedroom over the shop, just leaving a wardrobe that fitted into a niche in the wall, then placed two long tables and forms down the middle of the room. When the white tablecloths were on, things began to take shape. On the other side of the fireplace was a small half-cupboard on which was placed the wedding cake. The cake was made by a friend of Mum's, called Aunt Lou, no relation, but we all called her Aunt Lou. She had a fund of jokes and made us laugh; she worked at a place called Batgers. It was a work of art, made in two tiers, standing on four pillars, with little love birds on springs, horseshoes and little slippers, a little bride and groom on the top amid a cluster of flowers, and a lot of people came in to see it.

Saturday morning was all hands on deck. The neighbour from next door, a Mrs Adams, came in to see the cake. She looked at me and laughingly said, "Good heavens, are you the bride?"

I replied, "That's me."

I suppose I looked a mess, I had been very busy.

"You are now about to see a transformation." I then went through my usual routine, down to the baths, then across the way to the hairdresser, back home at last to get ready.

The day was windy, but dry. My sister was in the throes of getting ready, she was in her usual flap, so I helped her first. Bert and his sisters lived just a little way up the road, so, they would all be getting ready in their own house. Someone was sent to collect them.

Rose fixed my headdress so it would not blow off in the wind. Relations were arriving. There was a buzz of talk from downstairs, so time was getting near to go to the church.

Mum's Dad was waiting downstairs in the shop parlour and looking very spruce with his gold watch and chain across his chest. Frank, my eldest brother, would be giving me away, and was my witness. Henry, my third eldest brother, was to be the best man and was busy sorting out the guests. I couldn't help thinking about my father, Alphonso Bozza, who had passed away some seven years before. I would have loved to have had him walk me down the isle of our lovely church. He was on my mind that day as was the church of The Holy Name.

When it was my turn, there were people outside the house waiting to wish me all the best. I looked down the road towards Bert's house, and someone said, "He's waiting at the church", which caused a laugh and broke the tension for me. I was whisked away to church, and in no time was standing at the altar. It all seemed a dream. Bert was the only real thing, standing there beside me. Father Reardon did the service with his eyes closed, which made it seem more unreal. Bert looked at my face, and taking my hand he squeezed my fingers, which assured me it was for real. After signing the register, we were in the cars and away in no time at all. A welcome cup of tea was waiting for us. When we had all assembled, we made our way upstairs to our places at the table.

Someone had uncovered all the food, and tied a bunch of balloons full of confetti over the wedding cake. Names were on the table, so seating was easy. Bert and I stood up until everyone was seated, but when I sat down, someone had placed a whoopee cushion on my seat. Although I kept a stiff smile on my face, I thought it was in very bad taste. When I asked Bert if he knew it was there he said he would have removed it had he known. But that I was a very good sport, not to show my feelings, and perhaps it was meant for him.

The other thing about that day was Bert's Pop taking most of the photos one on top of the other, though we did get about six come out all right. It was that old box Brownie camera.

Bert had to go to work on Sunday, so Mum said you may as well stay here tonight, so our first night was spent in our respective homes.

When Sunday dawned, there was clearing up to be done. After we had put everything back in its place, we were ready to be off to 206 Sheppey Road, Dagenham.

Gathering up the rest of my belongings we were ready to go, and with the help of my brother Henry and his young lady, we set off. Two or three friends came to wave us off, and they jokingly said:
"What, no Honeymoon?"
I told them we were going to Bognor the first week in June, when we hoped the weather would be warmer. Seeing us off at the station, I told them not to forget to come and see us.

It was a nice feeling putting the key in my own door, and that I was here to stay at last. I set about making us a snack: dinner would be later, when Bert got in. Henry lit the fire, we later sat round it talking about the wedding.

We decided on the whole that things had gone very well. Bert's speech was a bit short, but sweet, he said he thought he was a very lucky man, and one wag said, "That remains to be seen."

We laughed at a few incidents such as Pop and the camera, and Henry had caught the back of his shoe on the running board, and it had come off. He had to get out of the car, and was nearly left behind. Although we knew Pop was having trouble with the camera, we didn't know what a fiasco it would be, although six were all right, and that was better than none at all.

We just showed Pop the half a dozen good ones.

Bert came home from work that Easter Sunday evening to a nice warm fire.

"Lovely," he said, with a big smile. I gave the Lord and Master his armchair. Henry said, "Lucky devil, we had better be going."

I thanked them for all their help, and waved them off from the porch.

I had lit a fire in the bedroom, as being newly built it seemed cold upstairs. We sat on the floor for a while in front of it talking, with Bert saying,
"Alone at last."

We climbed into bed.

I had kept my job at Daddy Harris's in the Mile End Road, so I travelled to Bow Road every day and walked the rest. Bert never knew where he would be working next, sometimes he was late home and others he was early. I liked him being there when I came in. It was very nice having the fire lit and perhaps the dinner on the go: being a naval man it all came easy to him.

Bert was late home more often than not. He sometimes stayed with his spreader until a job was complete. I did get used to it, although I was sometimes scared of being alone.

The evenings were getting lighter all the time, so I was able to poke around in the garden, which I loved doing.

Our week's holiday in Bognor Regis in the first week in June was lovely. We met some friends there, and thoroughly enjoyed ourselves. The week seemed to pass so quickly, but I must say we went back to work very refreshed from the rest.

Life went on in the same pattern for the next few months, when in July I became pregnant. When I told Bert he was as thrilled as I was. He thought I should give up work, but I said I would carry on for a couple of months.

But, sad to say, this was not to be. Something had gone dreadfully wrong. I was ill practically the whole of the first three months. Dr Finer of Woodward Road diagnosed a vesicular mole. I was four months when I was taken to Bartholomew's Hospital for a major operation. I remember being in there on Armistice Day.

Dr Finer was commended for his brilliant diagnosis.

I was told before I left hospital, that providing I waited two years, there was no reason why I could not have a perfectly healthy baby. Bert was on a job at Margate, but hurried home to fetch me. He wanted to see me ensconced comfortably in our little house. He knew I was still upset, and needed to be just us two. The operation had taken more out of me than I had expected, so it was quite a while before I could think of going back to work.

I cannot remember now if Ragusa Asphalt were slack or on strike, but Bert could not afford to be idle, so I thought seriously about going back to work. Bert said we'd manage, but my mind was made up though, so I contacted Daddy Harris. He said he didn't have the workshop in Mile End any more, and that he had gone to work in his son's factory in Aldgate, but his son would probably give me a job.

I had to think about this as Aldgate was a lot further than Bow. I decided to give it a try. Bert said if I thought I could do the journey, all well and good.

Meanwhile Bert said he would have a look down Fords. At that time they hadn't a good reputation, there were rumours that cameras were watching you all the time, and a chap called Smokey Joe, if he caught you smoking, would sack you at once, which they were always doing; anyway, he said it would not hurt to try. Bert managed to get a second-hand bike quite cheaply, and did a lot of work on it to make it roadworthy, but having got taken on that week, it got him from A to B.

I travelled to Aldgate. The trains were packed, and I never managed to get a seat, but when you are young, you take it all in your stride. After the first couple of weeks, the boss said that I would have to turn out a bit more work. I was a bit slow at first, but I soon picked up my usual speed, and Harris Junior acknowledged this.

Bert had been at Fords two and a half months. He was worried about the stories that were going round, rumours that a lot of men were being put off. Two hundred were put off the very next week. He was not among them. He kept his fingers crossed but he was among the next batch, the following week.

So Bert was out of work again.

His cousin Arthur Perkins heard about him being off work, and said he would ask for him at his firm. A week later he came to see Bert and said he had got an interview for him, but he warned him the money was very poor. Bert said he would take anything rather than be out of work. Bert was taken on for maintenance work at Marshall Taplows' wine and spirit department in Leytonstone, belonging to Charringtons. They were not known for their generosity in those days.

Bert thankfully liked the work and settled in. He used to get a train to Plaistow and walk to Leytonstone from there, to save a few coppers. The trains were electrified by that time. When Bert was working on Ashphalt his hands were all split and bleeding. I was glad to see they were much better now and vowed he would never go back to that kind of work again. The firm I worked for was called Harris and Goldberg and they were moving to bigger premises in Middlesex Street.

The building was called Industry House. When we had settled into the new place, I was made one of the supervisors, and looked after about thirty-six girls; some of these girls on piecework earned more than I did.

We were married three years when I miscarried. We were terribly upset. Dr Finer said that perhaps I should wait another two years. I burst out crying, saying, "I shall be an old woman before I have a baby."

He just sat there and laughed, saying "You are still young". Bert was as disappointed as I was. He said perhaps things are not quite right yet. At two and a half months, it is still a painful business.

We had made a very nice garden, with lawn down the middle and mostly roses and carnations in the borders, and a trellis on the outside edges, with roses trained along it. We spent a lot of time there relaxing, when we had finished gardening.

Bert had signed on to the Naval Reserve, so had to go each year to train. He was a Seaman Gunner. He went to Bisley on the firing range, I remember. He came home once with a medal and no towel; having given him one of my best towels, I was more concerned about my towel than his medal. We laughed about it later. Bert's eldest sister Dorothy and her husband Sid asked us if we would like to go to Cornwall with them. We said yes, we would like to, so we sorted out the appropriate week to suit all of us. Sid worked for the railways. He was in the offices so it never cost them much money. He had free passes, but he wasn't allowed to travel on the Cornish Express and we were, so they caught an earlier train, travelling from Essex. The journey seemed endless, but the scenery was fantastic. I came to love Cornwall and Devon, and we spent many happy holidays there. It was the farthest I had been, not speaking for Bert of course, who had been round the world with the Navy.

That holiday turned out truly wonderful in Cornwall.

We walked a lot, we also went fishing for mackerel, and went on climbing excursions with little parties of people. One was climbing Logan Rock. We climbed to the top. When the man said, "I want a volunteer to sit on the top" and the volunteers weren't forthcoming, one of the men grabbed me, and lifted me on the top. I didn't dare look down, the sea was bashing against the rocks far below; but that was not all – they began to move the rock gently from side to side.

I was glad when I was lifted down. I was saddened in later years that some students had pushed Logan Rock into the sea as a prank, and probably thought this very funny. I don't think it turned out quite so funny when they were made to hire a crane and pay to put it back, so incensed were the Cornish people about their famous landmark. We used to like having tea in a little café in St Ives. It consisted of a beautiful salad and a dish of crab, and it was eaten on a balcony looking out to the sea for sixpence. We would also enjoy sitting along the sea wall with the fishermen's wives, who were knitting while waiting for their men to come home from fishing with their catch to Mousehole Harbour. Then we would climb the steps, to the Ship Inn, to enjoy a drink with the locals.

We loved to walk from Penzance to Land's End and lie on the grass and watch the seagulls floating overhead. Happy days, the place is not the same now.

The next year we went to the Isle of Wight on our own. We had a very nice lodging near a golf course, called Wooton. A Mrs Pearce, a very nice person, was our landlady.

Talk about a small world. A friend of Mrs Pearce said she had seen Bert before, but could not recall where. Anyway they thought about it for a while, she had never been in our part of the country, so that made her think of all the places abroad she had been to. They came up with Singapore and Hong Kong.

"That's it!" she said. "You were a boarding party to take us to the ship where they were holding a tea dance for us."

Well you can imagine the reminiscences that started off. It must have been at least ten years before. We asked Mrs Pearce if we could stay on for the Bank Holiday weekend. She said yes, of course. We had a very relaxed and happy holiday there, which culminated in my being pregnant once more.

As soon as I was sure, I went to my doctor, and told him that I was prepared to put myself straight into his care.

We decided I must give up work. I would just finish out that week. My boss was surprised – he said other woman manage until they are six months or thereabouts. I said perhaps they don't have to stand in trains. When I explained further, he said he was sorry and hoped I would be all right. Bert got a half crown rise that week. I said things were looking up, and if they did that a little more often, we could live it up.

This is where my dressmaking skills came into their own. Bert said not to do too much, and I assured him that I wouldn't. As soon as it was known I was staying at home, I soon got some customers. I had to steer clear of the type of person who brought a piece of material saying, "I only paid three shillings and six pence for this", who was really saying that was all she wanted to pay for it to be made up, so I had to think about who I would make for and who I wouldn't. I didn't like artful people, because I never charged much anyway.

My sister had married the year previous to all this happening. She had a big wedding in Poplar Town Hall. She wed Jethro Farrant, a very nice chap from a very nice family. Jeff's three sisters and a little brother were her bridesmaids and page, and an elder brother his best man. They moved into two rooms in Bow, but were encouraged to do the same as we had done, and write to the council; being already married, they did not have to wait long, and they eventually they got a place quite near us.

My brother Richard was courting a girl named Florence, and when they married her name was the same as mine: Florence Bozza. I thought her rather nice. She had a nice smile. That year they had a little boy, and named him Francis (family name); we called him Frank.

He was a lovely little chap. Their second child was a little girl, whom they named Stella. She was brown haired, with lovely skin, and she was destined to be the mother of Sue Carpenter, a TV news reader.

They had a third baby they named Gwen, with light brown hair. This nice little family was now complete.

Richie as we called him was, at the time, working in the fish shop in Campbell Road called Nymans. People came from near and far to buy some, it was well known. Richie then left the fish shop to go and work in our aunt's shop, named Atterrano's, where they sold ice cream, sweets and cigarettes; it was in Angel Lane, Stratford.

It was when he was working for Aunt that he had an appendicitis attack. They rushed him into hospital, but before they could operate, it had turned into peritonitis.

Well, the hospital got him over this but warned him that he had to be very careful of his health.

But my brother did not take care of himself. He went out in any weather in a thin little jacket. He would go to the Bow Road Snooker Hall, rain or shine, so his general health deteriorated and within a very few weeks he was dead. My dear brother Richie. I remember his last words to me were, "Flo, don't come here again."

He worried about the poor soul in the bed opposite, who was using foul language. He then said, "Look out for my girls."

I would not have to break my journey to go to St Andrews Hospital, because my brother died that same night.

Because I lived in Dagenham and Richie's family lived in Bow it was not easy to look out for the children, but my brother Frank and his wife Nell, who had no children of their own, kept an eye on them; if any of the children weren't well, he sent them down to me.

My brother Frank sent Richie's little boy down to me when he was about three and a half. We had him for about ten days when he got a temperature. We took him to the doctor, who told us he had scarlet fever, so they put him in hospital, and took all my bedding away, and sealed up the room, which they did in those days. We slept in the little room on the floor. When they eventually brought it back, my new bedding was all scorched and the new blankets were all brown. I think I cried the whole of the time he was away. My sister Rose said,

"You cannot go and see him like that, you will make him worse". When I looked at his little clothes on the line blowing in the wind I blubbered again. When he said he wanted to go back to his auntie's, they told him he would get the fever again, because he kept crying.

Bert and his little nephew had such fun over in Castle Green playing football, and asked if he was coming back: I said his mum wouldn't let him.

My brother told me afterwards that the two boys upstairs where he lived had gone away with it, so he must have caught it off them, and it was lucky the two girls had not caught it too. Later when his sister Gwen wasn't well, my brother Frank, ever watchful, sent Gwen to me. She had fallen over and had sore knees and elbows. I knew my brother Frank and his wife Nell always worried over Richie's children, but I soon had her patched up and well again.

She stayed about three weeks, and when I took her home, Frank and Nell said I had done a good job on Gwen. She looked a different girl. When evacuation was on, we lost touch with Frank, Stella and Gwen. My brother Frank said he thought they were sent to Swindon, and that they were all sent to the same place, but it was ages after that he found out where they were. Their mother liked having the place to herself so she never kept us informed.

The eldest boy Frank stayed in Swindon and never did come home. He finally married a Swindon girl, and had one daughter named Deborah; we never knew any of this at the time, as the war messed a good many of our lives up; six years was an awfully long time.

My sister Rose had had a little boy in September, Jethro junior. It was nice to walk with her to the shops, with her little boy in his pram. I was looking forward to doing the same. April could not come quickly enough! Christmas came and went, we spent some of the time at my sister's, and some at our house.

We were afraid to buy a pram or anything much. We didn't want to put the cart before the horse as the saying goes. I had reached February feeling pretty good, with two more months to go. I had been on tenterhooks till now, but at seven months was much calmer. I knew baby was all right and kicking; in those days you never knew the sex but didn't care either way.

Our little girl was born on the twenty-second of April. When Bert came in to see her, he said, "She is like a little rabbit". I, like all mums the world over, thought she was beautiful, although she did have bits of cotton wool stuck all over her, and no eyebrows. When I got to look at others, I still thought she was tiny but the best in my eyes.

Pamela Morgan did all the usual things babies do, such as teething, crawling, and walking by the time she was one year old. I daresay she was also spoiled, there was an excuse for us – we had waited so long, or so it seemed, for a baby. I was twenty-six years old and Bert was thirty-seven. I thought we were old but perhaps it was because I had wanted to have four children. My sister did everything right, because she managed it. Jethro and Pam were good playmates even though he was a little older.

Bert came home from work one day and said, "I can book a week's holiday in Yarmouth. A chap at work has given me an address to write to."

I said, "When, Bert?"

"July all right, Flo?"

"That will be fine, Pamela will be one year three months, just right." So Bert went ahead and booked.

The holiday was confirmed and when the time drew near, Bert said, "Got everything?"

I was packed all except for Pamela's shoes. She only took size one, and firm soles started at size two, they were too big, but she couldn't walk around in soft soles on holiday. Bert said not to worry, see what we can get in Yarmouth, and with that we went to catch the coach.

Our lodgings were a nice little house, one of a row with long gardens in front. Most of them had vegetables growing in them. We had a nice room in the house and made ourselves comfortable. The owners were likeable folk and we quickly became friends; they were a mother and her two sons who were fishermen.

I cannot recall their names now, but what I do remember was how worried she was for her sons. Looking to Bert for a reassurance that he couldn't give, "Mr Morgan," she would say, "do you think there will be a war? Do you think my two sons will have to go?"

Bert would smile at her and say something like, "I sincerely hope not, because if there is a war, I will be one of the first to go." Then he would joke about how they would be needed to provide food and probably be OK. This poor worried mum thought because Bert was a Naval Reservist, he somehow had privileged information. I really felt for her and her two fine sons.

Bert and I had a lovely time in Yarmouth during our stay with them. We went around the markets, sampled the tripe and other tasties offered. I can honestly say I do not like tripe.

Our little daughter Pam loved the beach, all those stretches of sand – and she played on a narrow row of stones. I had made her a mustard coloured coat, tailored with a half belt and a brown velvet collar. She was so tiny. Passers-by would say, "What a lovely little boy..." so Bert and I went and bought her a sweet little bonnet, and managed to find a rare pair of size one baby shoes with a proper sole. We thought this was a great find.

We returned home to our house in Dagenham after a very enjoyable holiday in Yarmouth and vowed we would return to see our new-found friends again. I have often thought of that poor woman, and what it must have been like for her along with the rest of us, as a very short time after our holiday, all the rumours about war came true. Bert was called up two weeks before war was declared. As he went, he said to me with a reassuring smile,
"I'll take the front door key Flo; you'll see, I'll probably be home by the weekend."

He was thinking (and hoping) it would be a false alarm. We did have a scare the year before.

As it turned out, when he arrived at Chatham Barracks and lined up for his kit, a chap called out, "Morgan, down this end."

There were a series of wire cages set out and you had to pass through them, they were all in rows. Bert said he was really surprised when he was directed to a cage that was giving out whites.

Tropical whites meant foreign service. He knew then that he wouldn't be going home at the weekend, or for a good many more weekends to come.

Everything happened quickly after that. Bert found himself on a train with others, which was taking them to the ferry. Here, all the civilians were turned off to make room for naval personnel. They crossed to France where a train was waiting for them. Bert told me a long time afterwards that they were on this train for three days and were unable to wash or shave, and beginning to look a bit of a mess. The train was non-stop.

When it did stop, they found that their next mode of transport was waiting for them at Marseille. It was a flying boat, which was going to take them to join their ship the *H M S Arethusa*. They knew she was somewhere in the Mediterranean.

I never knew for a long time where Bert was, but my very first taste of war came when my sister Rose and I were standing in her garden. We had been talking about the food we were going to need to grow during the war to feed our families, when three planes suddenly came really low over the tops of the houses. They were so big and a darkish grey colour, you could see every detail and the markings on the sides of them. We quickly realized that these were enemy planes and the direction they were going meant they were on their way back across the River Thames to their own country.

Call it woman's intuition, but I just felt, I instinctively knew that this wasn't a bombing raid party, and that they had probably seen what they had come for, met up and were flying home together over the English Channel. Such was the confidence of the enemy in the beginning that it was enough to throw all around in panic.

Rosie started screaming and neighbours appeared from all corners. The sirens started and we all ran for the dug-outs, most of us in one, all crammed in. We said our prayers.

I think my intuition was right, and these planes weren't dropping bombs but I felt very uneasy as this time, these planes were well ahead of our warning system.

This is when I really felt the great separation and lack of news from my dear Bert. They might only have been on a reconnaissance, but this was for real, and the feeling was awful.

It is true to say that the best sides of people come out in times of adversity.

We used to get lots of advice via the radio, such as, do not forget to stock your shelter with candles and don't cut that string, untie the knot, and save it, and don't forget the blackout.

Our present Queen spoke to us through the radio, she said:
"Margaret Rose and I feel for the families who have to leave their homes, the children being evacuated, whose only identity is the ticket tied to them – I call for all woman to have fortitude at this time."

It was later that we learned that Churchill, that great man who was to lead us through the war, had ordered that tanks be strategically placed along the banks of the River Thames. There were hundreds of them, all dummies, made of rubber and other substances, and they were designed to fool the enemy so that they never knew our real strength. In later years my children along with their friends played on a few remaining ones.

As the months passed I was overjoyed one morning to receive a letter from Bert. The first one. Of course I knew he wouldn't be able to say much, but I was so grateful to hear from him at long last that the feeling of elation lasted for some time. On the envelope it said – Sans Origin.

When I think of the way I searched a map of the world for this place... until I finally realized it meant, nowhere. Fancy me thinking it would have a destination! I felt a prize fool, and me a sailor's wife.

Meanwhile evacuation was going on. Rose was about to have her second baby, so she was sent to Bishop's Stortford. I was being sent to Bradford on Avon, and taking my daughter, and Rosie's little boy Jethro and my mother. The train we were put on going to Bradford on Avon was jammed full of mothers, grandmothers, children, some crying, some asleep. It was a traumatic time for everyone.

Little Jethro was only two years and a few months old, just old enough to realize something was very wrong. Not so my Pamela, one and a half years, and she had her mum.

When we eventually arrived at Bradford on Avon, we were met by a parson who took us all to a church hall. Here there were some of his women helpers and they tried to sort the evacuees out, and place them with homes that offered to help.

As there were four of us and we wouldn't agree to be split up, nobody readily seemed to want us, and after a long wait, everyone else seemed to have been accommodated and I was wishing we had stayed at home and taken our chance.

There was a largish woman who came in a bit late saying she had one room. The parson asked me if I could manage with one bed, and I said I didn't think I could manage for very long in one bed. I was smartly told by the woman that there was a war on and I would have to manage or go without.

To be told in this cold manner, here in this place that we had been sent to, with two small children to care for, that there was a war on, was like twisting the knife, with my own husband away at sea, and ships going down every day with losses of hundreds of lives.

And us here, because we lived in a high risk target area. I certainly didn't need to be told by her that there was a war on. I held my tongue. These people were well paid for us, and she had four in one room. I'm sure she could have borrowed a camp bed, making our plight a little easier.

I know if the position had been reversed, it would have been a different story, and we would have bent over backwards for these people.

I was glad to have my mother with me, she was such a tower of strength, and so patient and resilient. We hired a pushchair. Mother used to take the two children to the park. Thank goodness the weather remained good. I cooked and cleaned and got the washing up to date before joining them.

I had a letter from Bert. He was terribly worried about us all, and wondered if we were getting enough to eat, and how the rations were working out. Goodness knows what the men had been hearing. I wrote straight back, to put his mind at rest. I had no idea how he received our letters, or how long they took.

My sister Rose wrote to say she was now home, and had another little boy and was going to call him Frank. It appears she was missing little Jethro and was worrying herself sick, and could Mum bring him home as things didn't seem too bad at the moment.

I put Mum and little Jethro on a coach, and we kissed them good-bye. Jeff senior met them at the other end, and said how well they looked, and spending a lot of time in the fresh air had done them good.

After one more week in Bradford, I decided to take my Pam home as well. I thanked the large women for making a room available in her house for us, and knew I would be just glad to get home, but my sister's husband wouldn't hear of me staying in my house and insisted I live with them, where we'd all be together. He told me he had promised Bert he would look out for us. Jeff was a riveter in the docks and a fire-fighter at home. I agreed. My own little house was only just around the corner, two streets away.

Ready to join in the First World War.

Survivors of HMS Glatton.

Heavy Cruiser Squadron, Baltic, First World War.

Ship's concert party.

Greek refugees being taken aboard, 1920s.

HMS Cambrian divers.

Aboard HMS Verity.

Return of landing parties from raiding pirate lairs along Yanzte River, China.

Torpedo tube, HMS Cambrian.

HM Aircraft Carrier Hermes, June 3rd, 1925.

HMS Diomede, Durban and despatch, 1923.

HMS Hermes, China station, Amoy.

Graves of British victims, Yokohama, Japan.

HMS Arethusa landing parties.

HMS Arethusa landing party, World War Two.

Ark Royal escort under attack HMS Arethusa.

So that's how we lived for the time being, settled down with Rose and her growing family. My daughter and I in their small bedroom and them sharing the big bedroom. Jeff junior in his little single bed, baby in a cot in the corner of their room.

We tilled the garden together along with the neighbours – it was called 'Growing for the homefront' and strange to say now, I actually enjoyed it. We vigilantly patched our blackout curtains, and generally looked out for each other. We all worked together – even the government did with a coalition party that trained all their thoughts, wits and efforts, as one, to get us through this terrible war.

Rose's little Jeff and my Pam were good playmates and filled their days with just that, play. Her Francis was an exceptionally good baby, so things for the most part ran smoothly.

It was a few months after war was declared that we were issued with gas masks. Pam's was a Mickey Mouse face with a pink tongue, with straps around the back of the head. We took the threat seriously and tried them out several times, but thank the Lord, we never had to use them; these were frightening times for us mums.

Women were being conscripted into industry. I knew of some that were taking the place of the men. Women worked on all jobs and any jobs, and did a good job, as good as the men in some cases. They also worked on the land, drove lorries and tractors; they dug potatoes brought in the harvest, and were known as the Land Army Girls; in fact, women took on a new role in life.

I remember the fuss some men made because Upminster Common was to be dug up to grow food.

After the war there was a bitter struggle to get it put back to being Upminster Common again for the people, and the people won in the end. I was pleased about that because it was one of our favourite venues. A very pretty place.

We had some cheery rousing tunes, songs that lifted our spirits during those grey days. Songs like, 'We'll Meet Again'; 'The White

Cliffs of Dover'; 'Pack Up Your Troubles'; 'Down Forget-Me-Not Lane'; 'Live and Love Another Day'; 'Run Rabbit Run'; 'Roll Out the Barrel', and heaps more. Some of the entertainers were, Vera Lynn, Ann Shelton, Arthur Askey, Gracie Fields, Max Bygraves, Bob Hope, and many more. I hope these people knew how much they helped us to bear being parted from our men, who were away fighting for our country.

A lot of the neighbours who had grown up children or no family worked in the factories making components for our armies, so we sometimes helped with their productive gardens. In fact, garden fences almost disappeared as we juggled the chores of the day. I never knew it before, and I've never felt it since, but the friendship and the comradeship that we had for each other was boundless.

You cannot imagine the satisfaction of digging up buckets full of Arran Pilot potatoes, and sharing them with the neighbours. I will never forget the size or the flavour of those potatoes.

Our mother made the occasional visit from the East End to see us, and put her mind at rest that we were coping. My brother-in-law, Jeff, was an electric welder and had as much work as he could handle, as you can imagine, and being in the home guard was kept very busy, sometimes to the point of exhaustion. His father before him had been a welder, and had won a countrywide prize for being the fastest known riveter on warships in the First World War. His name was Mr Farrant.

Although we did not know what was happening to Bert, evidently he was in the thick of things. His light cruiser, the *Arethusa*, was on convoy duty. This meant they cruised alongside the convoy of ships taking supplies, medical, food, and lots that we didn't know of then, escorting them as safety as they could. But it was a sad fact that we lost a lot of ships like this as they were constantly bombed from the air and torpedoed. It was just as well we didn't know just how bad things were until much later.

By this time, my brother Albert had married Vera, and my brother Henry was suddenly taken ill and went into St Andrews Hospital,

Bow. He was nursed back to health by Grace, whom he fell in love with and later married. Grace was exactly as her name, and we all loved her. They soon had a bonny bouncing pair of twin girls called Ann and Carol, with big blue eyes and blonde curls. Then came Roger, then Judy, with dark hair and Italian-looking. Then, in the thick of the war, in their dark damp cramped dugout, another pair of twins were born to Grace and Henry. Twin girls, Jean and Beryl. How we worried about them all, but Grace never complained once, and took it all in her stride.

Grace had come from quite a well-to-do family, and her sister Elsie, who had been her bridesmaid, played the violin in the philharmonic orchestra.

As money was very tight, I made Grace's wedding dress and those of the bridesmaids as well. Our present to them. Their first home was the fruit shop, now no longer used as this and closed down. Later they moved to a little shop a few doors down that had housed a tailor. They sold all kinds of bric-a-brac here, and made a real go of it. I can see now their twins (one each end) of my Pam's pram that we had given them. Fortunately I had been impetuous and at the time bought a really big boat pram! It now answered their needs admirably.

They had one more child, Christopher, which completed that family. Thinking of the family now, it's a good job we can't see round the corner of life, as when Jean and Beryl were just seventeen, Beryl and her boyfriend were going to get engaged and save for their marriage, so he was going to sell his motorbike that weekend. As a last time, they did a 'ton up' I think it was called, on the Southend Road, and were unable to pull out of a bend and were both killed. Beryl was killed outright and he lived for fifteen minutes on the grass verge with a passing motorist holding his hand. Beryl had been catapulted a very great distance.

The youngsters had a double funeral and were buried in the same grave in the Catholic cemetery in Leytonstone. They had a huge following, and many youngsters from their places of work came. They were a well-liked couple. The wreaths were endless, some done like enormous gramophone records.

It made me remember my father's funeral. My brother and his wife were inconsolable, and the family stayed in a state of shock and mourning for a long time.

I was still living with Rose and Jeff. A few months went by before Bert was granted a few days' leave. By this time Pam was copying little Jethro and called Jeff daddy. We kept telling her to say uncle but she would soon forget. I knew Bert would be hurt, so I had a picture of Bert enlarged and hung it on the wall. Every night Pam would kiss Daddy Bert goodnight before she went to sleep. This had the desired effect and when he came home she made a great fuss of him, and didn't want him to go back. Neither did I.

My brother Henry and his wife Grace were looking forward to the time when they would be re-accommodated in a new flat, and their very old house was to be pulled down. An indoor toilet would be a luxury, also a bathroom, and a modern kitchen. Meanwhile, Henry was working for the railway, as a night watchman. He had a little hut with a telephone, and was to guard the goods in the railway yards.

Everything went along smoothly for a couple of years, when suddenly one dark night, Henry spotted four men moving around. He had an arrangement with his wife Grace that when he spoke to her on the phone, if he used unfamiliar words she was to phone the police. Well, Grace did this at once, and the police were soon on the scene, but not before the men had fired a shot at Henry. The shot was so close that Henry was in shock for a couple of days.

Grace was also in shock – she wanted Henry to find a safer job. He was off work for quite some time, but knowing my brother I knew he would soon find a job.

A couple of years later they were comfortably housed in a downstairs flat in Woodford, with two bedrooms, a very nice bathroom, a lounge and kitchen – such a change from their old house in Bow.

Meanwhile, I was patiently waiting for Bert's leave.

It was lovely to see Bert. He looked quite well considering. Sometimes people would ask him what it was like out there. He would never discuss the war, but what he did tell us were little snippets about his time in China and Hong Kong during his twelve years as a signed up sailor. Bert would hold us spellbound with the stories.

Like when he and a fellow sailor were leaning over the side of their ship anchored in the harbour in China. There was a large water population then, as on land there was overcrowding, when they saw a toddler fall from one of the sanpans, into the water. When nobody seemed to notice, they climbed over the side, down the rope ladder and his shipmate swam over and put the child back onto the sanpan. Bert helped him up onto the boat, and they were about to go below when they saw the child being put back into the water. They went in for the child again and this time brought the baby back to the ship. He became the captain's errand boy. They learned that the parents would assume the water god had called the child, and would never retrieve it back once it had fallen in.

Also, girls were not a popular baby, and were usually floated out on a plank and left as soon as they were born.

We were sorry to see him go back to sea. Mother had married a man named George Webb, he was about ten years younger than Mum, and had been in submarines in the First World War. George was a quiet man and kept himself to himself, but they got along all right. He never minded her coming to see us but rarely came himself.

On some particularly concentrated bombing raids in the centre of London and the outskirts, Mum and George were bombed out, twice, in Stepney Green. Something had to be done, so I told Rose and Jeff I had better go home now and take Mum and George with me to live, and so they moved in with me. Mum was upset at her home being such a mess of rubble, but was happy to be with us in Dagenham.

Our dug-out (called an Anderson Shelter), was now a regular part of our lives. Almost every night now the sirens would go. We knew as darkness fell, that we would hear that sickening drone of enemy planes, loaded with a wicked cargo, and as we trundled to the shelter we would be silently wondering who would they be dropped on this time. We all had good reason to feel scared, and my poor mother would fear for all our lives.

I remember one clear night when we were all huddled in the shelter. We had only just settled down when a bomb went off so close to us that we were all thrown about, and some of the earth fell in on us.

I told Mum I must go and see who had been hit, it had to be a neighbour, and I had to see if there was anything I could do to help. So with shaking legs I climbed out of the dug-out and wedged the door back tightly closed. Going through my house to the front door I found it had been blown off and nearly all our windows were broken. I ran down the road towards the huge plume of black smoke. About eight houses down from mine, two houses had completely disappeared.

The gas main was alight so we could see clearly. Both families were in their dug-outs, shaken but all safe and accounted for. We all decided nothing could be done until morning. When I told Mum, we both said thank God they are all safe this time.

The enemy were always aiming for the railway lines. One time they did hit the lines, and it lifted them over the tops of the houses, into the street on the other side of the railway. No one was hurt, not one single casualty, a miracle no less. How proud I was of the British people, the way they worked then; in a few short hours they were laying new lines. All was up and running like oiled wheels. I still think it was amazing.

At this rate, the enemy would never beat us. We were all very encouraged.

At one time when I had some damage after a bomb had dropped a little way up the street, there were broken windows and some of the glass was stuck in the piano, and of course the net curtains were torn, and in the kitchen, a little door in the wall of the chimney was blown open, and there was soot everywhere. Unlucky for me the table was laid and there was soot in the sugar, the butter, and all over the bread – soot everywhere. I did not know where to start! I contacted the council. They sent some men to put windows in, and mend the door. The men were rushing around, as you can guess they were very busy. It was not until a long while after that I found out I could have had money for spoilt food and rations. Also, more importantly, I could have had new nets for the windows, but at the time I never knew any of this.

Yet there were people who had practically no damage that pretended to have any amount of things spoilt. As I had done a lot of the clearing up myself and changed my net curtains I decided not to join the queue. I always lost out, in those circumstances. But to be honest, I was thankful that I still had a roof over my head. Things that happened to me were minimal, while some poor devils had lost everything.

I heard one day about some old neighbours who had lived near us in Campbell Road: they had had a direct hit on their Anderson shelter, and the man and wife were killed, and the old father who had hidden in a cupboard was saved, although very shaken up. I can imagine that poor man with his son and daughter-in-law dead. I was always doubly shocked if I knew the people that these awful things had happened to.

But we had a saying, 'soldier on', and this we tried to do despite everything.

I went round Rosie's to tell her. She could see from my face that I was upset, and we commiserated together.

Later, I was to despair. At the top of my road was the Station, Becontree. The people used to pour out of the trains when the air raids sounded and go into the communal shelters alongside the station. The shelter had a direct hit, two hundred people dead and very few survivors.

This plummeted our spirits. Even lower still when our dear St Anne's Catholic Church was hit, killing two nuns.

One day during the war I had a young lady call on me and ask if I could make some overalls for the girls that worked at May and Baker. They were famous for their May and Baker tablets. I told her I would, and a roll of green material was delivered a few days later.

The work girls came in ones and twos to be measured; I suppose I made a couple of dozen overalls in all until the material ran out. Perhaps their usual supplier had been bombed, and they had to look around for machinists to make them. I don't think that I was the only one working on them. The material was hard to come by – everything was on coupons – but I was glad to help them out. We never spoke about what we were doing, in fact there were posters on railway station walls and other places saying, 'Be Like Dad And Keep Mum'. We were told that even walls have ears, so we never told anyone anything.

About every two months Bert would send me a five shilling postal order. He earned it dobieing (that's washing garments for the officers). He would get tuppence or a threepenny joey, a piece. Bert would say, "Get yourself a coat to keep warm or anything you need." I didn't remind him that I would need the clothes coupons to go with this. I was happy to save this until Bert would come home, and hoped we could spend it on our future.

A few months had passed and I hadn't heard from Bert when I saw a telegram boy in the usual outfit of red and a pillbox hat, lean his cycle against my privet and walk up the path to my door. I froze.

After a few agonising seconds, I was leaping about the house with joy. Bert's ship, the *Arethusa*, would be docking for a short while and would I go to Sheerness where Bert would be granted a few hours' shore leave. So me, Pam and Mum set off with great excitement. My little daughter was a bundle of energy: now she was to see again her Daddy Bert in the flesh, instead of the picture she kissed every night.

When we arrived at Sheerness, of course, there were crowds upon crowds of people already there. Police were linked arm in arm keeping the people back. We had only been there a short while when a shout went up:

"Here they come."

Everyone seemed to surge forward and the police were having a job to hold them back. Mum and I had somehow got quite near the front and were stretching our necks to see, when Pam slipped my hand and dived under the policemen's legs and was gone, running as fast as her legs would carry her. I shouted, then screamed at her to come back and tried to go after her but it was hopeless.

Sailors were pouring off the platform towards us. I looked down at the policemen's legs and was thinking of doing the same as my daughter when a policeman turned round and nodded his head in the direction of the sailors, saying, "Is that your little girl?"

Halfway down the platform, I could see her bobbing along on someone's shoulder. It had been a scary few moments for Mum and I, but somehow Pam had found her Dad. The Daddy Bert picture had paid off.

How the navy managed it, I do not know, but we were all together as a family for two and a half hours. A little time is better than none. We felt we all deserved it.

Back at home that night, Pam told Grandad George all about it. We gave him the proper version later. He could not believe it. He had told Pam, "they didn't do things like that in my navy", and of course, she wanted to know all about his navy. We laughed when he raised his eyes to the ceiling, telling himself he'd brought it on himself.

An old school friend, Mary, now lived next door but one with her husband Harry and their children Pat and Brian. Mary and I had become very close friends and neighbours. One day, late in the afternoon, the sirens went off quite unexpectedly. We could already hear the enemy planes before leaving the house. Mum wanted to sit under the stairs with her apron over Pam's head (who was quite happy to stay there) but I insisted we all go to the shelter as usual, and hurried them out the back door, watching them climb into the dug-out.

I looked across the garden and saw Mary waving frantically and pointing to a train coming at full speed with an enemy plane right behind it flying really low. It started machine-gunning it and we could see the white flashes from the gunner. It had been raining earlier, and the path was very slippery. Mum and Pamela had made it safely, and I ran after them.

I could see the neighbour on the other side of Mary running up her garden with a saucepan on her head, and a tin box under her arm. I smiled as Mrs Coleman did look comical, although we all kept saucepans in the garden for emergencies. I could hear Mary shouting,
"Are you down, Flo? Are you down, Flo?" I was down all right, I had fallen flat in the mud. Above me in the sky a tremendous dog fight was going on, between us and enemy planes. The planes were swinging in circles and dipping and climbing with bursts of gun fire. I called to Mary, "I'm down all right, down here in the mud."

Mary hopped across the gardens like a youthful hurdler and yanked me to my feet. I was mud spattered and angry.
"Its a good job your Bert can't see you!" she shouted above the noise. Mary had black shoulder length hair, and she resembled Margaret Lockwood, a beautiful actress of our era, with a beauty spot as well.

She plonked my saucepan on my head, and did likewise with hers. We looked up and we both shouted obscenities, shaking our fists.

The Anderson shelter was very damp. I didn't relish the thought of spending the night there, but we were lucky this time, as the all clear went two hours later. I felt lucky to have Mary and Harry living close, they were great. They both worked on the buses, mostly on the same bus and sometimes had the route that took them near the river Thames, past a pub that was called the Ship and Shovel. This was about a mile from where we lived. One day during an air raid, a bomb dropped near. A short while after I could hear Mary's voice calling me:

"Flo, it seemed to be over this way, I think it was over Robin Hood Way!"

I said, "Keep calm Mary, everything is all right. Have you time for a cuppa?"

"Where are the children?"

I said, "They have taken Pamela round Rosie's. I am going round to join them presently."

Mary was agitated because of what she had seen – it looked as if it was in our direction – and wanted to know if I knew where it had fallen; she was always on tenterhooks about the children.

I knew she was on a shift.

I calmed her down and said I wasn't sure, and started to make her a cup of tea, asking if she had finished for the day as she was in her conductress uniform. Mary suddenly jumped up.

"Flo, I've left Harry with the bus at the Ship and Shovel." She'd only wanted to see that her children were all right (they had been in my garden) and she was off running down the road.

Apparently she had jumped off the bus telling Harry she had to see if the kids were all right, and run all the way home. When she got back to the bus, Harry had been entertaining the passengers with some card tricks while they waited. They carried on with their journey as if it was an everyday normal event...

Mary was so fit and always rushing about, like the morning we were both hanging washing out.

"Do you think it's going to rain, Flo?" she called across the garden. Mary was in her uniform and hanging washing out as fast as she could.

She sometimes came in on her way to work, or more often than not on her way home like this particular day. At the end of her shift a knock at the door brought my chirpy friend in, saying, "Look how I went to work today Flo." Mary unbuttoned her coat to reveal her apron with a pocket full of pegs.

She was always making me laugh, and lifting my spirits because she knew how much I worried with all the ships going down, and no news from Bert for quite a while now.

Like the time she told me about her route through London in the rush hour on the old red double decker twenty-threes. She always began the same way.

"What about this then Flo... lunch time in Oxford Street. I had 'em standing inside, upstairs, everywhere. When we stopped I put my arm across, before anyone from the queue could jump on. I'm full up, full up. This bloke rushed out of the queue. 'Let me on.' I said, I've got no more room, mate, sorry. Get off. He was hanging on the pole on the platform of the bus. 'Let me on. You must let me on, I'm the Rabbi.' I don't care if you're bloody Popeye, I said, I'm full up..."

Or the time when she had this cheeky teenager smoking his head off downstairs in the bus.

"What's the matter with you this morning, can't you read, sonny?" pointing to a no smoking sign.

"Na lady, I went to night school, I can't read in the daytime."

"I clipped his ear, Flo, and sent him upstairs."

She and Harry sometimes took the bus across London when the blitz was on, bumping over the rubble. Harry told her to clip the tickets as near the edge as possible on this journey – (in those days the conductor had a wooden ticker rack about a foot long with little piles of different coloured tickets all along it, held by wire clips, each denoting a different price by colour, you took one out and put it in a small silver machine which hung around your neck and rested on your chest, pressed the lever and it punched a hole in the side of the ticket) – most people threw their tickets on the floor of the bus.

At the end of the journey, Harry collected all the tickets from the floor, and while they were on their break in the café, he cut all the sides of the tickets off and put them back in Mary's rack. I knew this was for some good cause or other. As Mary said:

"You know Flo, when the devil drives..." then had a good laugh at her own pun.

Back at the garage, they had to pick up more tickets. They were always helping others and I remember them with great warmth. Especially the time we had a do in a hall at the top of our road. Harry got up and entertained the whole crowd by singing a love song in Spanish. He had everyone enthralled and held his audience spellbound. At the end, we said, "Harry that was wonderful, we didn't know you could speak Spanish." He said he couldn't and had made it all up... he was so convincing. I bet there was no one there who knew, except me and Mary of course.

Weeks were growing into months when out of the blue I received a telegram from Bert. His ship had had to come into dock in Newcastle. He was at Hebburn on Tyne and was coming home right now to take us back with him for a month.

We had to be ready to leave straight away as he was on a twenty-four hour pass. I had a case with my and Pam's things in record time and practically before I could turn round, he was home, smiling his old smile.

Bert said he had arranged some lodgings with very nice people. Mum was anxious to know how long we would be gone and Bert told her that he had a month's leave coming up. Mother was happy for us, but speechless.

It had all been a bit quick.

I had made our little daughter a very nice blue nylon fur coat and beret. We set off. Poor Bert, I should have realized. We hadn't gone very far before Bert was covered in bits of fur, I should have given it a good brush.

On the train we had a chance to talk and he could see my eyes were full of questions. He said, as he looked me straight in the eye, "The main thing is that you know I'm OK, but our ship has been holed in the side, big enough to get one of Harry and Mary's buses in."

Bert could see it was a shock, but as he said, I knew he was all right. He said it might even take a couple of months to repair. He assured me they wouldn't be sending him anywhere else in the meantime.

I was eager to know all about our lodgings. Bert told me how he went out of the shipyard into a little public house the other evening for a break to get away from the repair work noise, and spent a few minutes watching the locals play darts before returning to the needs of the ship, when he got chatting to some locals who invited him to play a game of darts with them. While playing darts, one of the men asked him if he was off the *Arethusa*. Bert said yes, he was. The chap then said, "You don't sleep aboard her, do you?" Bert said, yes he did. Then without hesitation this man said, you had better come home with me, if you've got time for a bite of supper. My Peggy won't mind."

Bert took up this offer, and evidently Peggy wouldn't hear of him sleeping aboard, with 'all that din going on', as she put it. Peggy said, "You must fetch your wife and little girl here."

It was before five next morning when we arrived to find the door slightly ajar. Also, a big bedroom, and as we went in on the right it had a big fire blazing in the hearth. It had obviously been made ready for us. It looked very welcoming indeed.

I was never so glad to fall into bed. It was mid-morning before I met Peggy. I liked her instantly and her little girl was a couple of months younger than ours.

As it turned out, it was very nice for them to be playmates. Pam was very outgoing and made herself at home straight away.

I told Peggy how grateful to her I was for inviting us into their home, and wanted to help with the work and cooking. She readily handed the cooking over to me and we got on really well.

I can honestly say we were truly happy with Jack and Peggy Diamond – they were the sort of people you didn't come across often, and Bert had been lucky enough to come across them. Peggy would go into raptures over my pastry and I was very flattered. She would joke, "I thought you Londoners lived out of tins." I told her there weren't many tins in my house. Well, not with me and my mum in the house.

The trouble was, the position of the big table I used to roll the pastry out on meant I had my back to the great big fire. I used to sweat buckets. If the sirens went off, Jack would come dashing in for his tin helmet, put us all in the shelter, then go rushing off. But strange to say, now, I don't remember this happening very often while up there.

Bert took us and the children to Newcastle to the pictures. We saw *Desert Song*. Seeing it all that time ago we thought it was lovely. It took us into another world, and let us forget the war briefly.

The crew of *H M S Arethusa* gave a party aboard ship for all the wives and children of the crew. There was still plenty of noise from the welders and other workmen, but the children didn't seem to notice.

I can remember plenty of little jellies and cakes and tea. Everyone had worked very hard, and I thought how nice it was of the sailors to do it.

For me it was a thrill to be on the *Arethusa* where Bert had spent so much of his time away from us. I tried not to think of the hole in her side, and thanked God she had been lucky so far.

Bert put Pam on his shoulders and took her to see part of the engine room. There were large wheels that went round and seemed to drive enormous type pistons up and down and the smell of engine oil and grease and the heat and noise made me feel queasy, but I wasn't going to miss anything. The inner ship was a surprise to me, much bigger than I had imagined. Seeing the mounted guns, even though they were covered up, made an impression on me and I could imagine them circling around, sounding off, following aircraft.

The men and officers were an impressive sight to see. Efficient and immaculate. It was hard to imagine these same smiling men as dogs of war. Everywhere on the ship looked freshly painted and clean. Bert had often joked, if it didn't move, paint it.

The men had a rotating shift, half the men on, and half off, then change shift. Time was getting near now for Bert's proper leave. These few weeks had flown and now it was going to be hard to say good-bye to our new-found friends, so kind. We couldn't thank them enough.

We caught the train to London, then got the connection to Dagenham and were soon walking down our road to our little house. I could see quite clearly my mother's smiling face from a long way off: Pamela was away, arms outstreched ready to give her the usual strangle hold. I heard mother say, "Come and tell Nanny all about it."

Bert's leave (exactly one month) was spent visiting relatives and friends. For a lot of the time I agonised and secretly worried about his return to the ship, but I was determined to see that we made the most of his leave. I baked, and cooked his favourites, as far as rations would allow, and we spent time with his three sisters and his brother Bill and family, and Rose and Jeff.

We fitted a lot into a short time. Everyone wanted to see him and know about his experiences at sea. Mum used to say, "Where are you off to today then?" and we would tell her our latest jaunt.

Evenings found us all gathered around, while Bert would relate a snippet here and there, and we would all inwardly digest a slice of the war from his view.

Portsmouth was the Royal Navy's base, and from there the escort ships looked after the convoy, keeping the supply routes open, at the same time looking out for enemy battleships. During bombardment, the ship's gunners on deck would be locked into the gun turrets.

They would talk of our Battle of Britain planes, the Spitfire and Hurricanes based at Chichester and what a grand job they were doing, and such things as the well known latest developed Mulberry Harbours and Pluto pipelines, now hurriedly being built at Southampton and laid from the Isle of Wight to Cherbourg. Great concrete sections, it seemed the South and South West were one huge assembly point.

Someone asked Bert if he know where this secret place was supposed to be that was assembling submarines before they were taken for their sea trials on the Solent. If he knew, he wasn't saying, he just started talking about the years in-between the wars, and did we remember the great Hussars? The cavalry, such a magnificent sight. Sad when the cavalry exchanged their horses for machines and the Great Royal Hussars became armoured cars.

Bert had a Chinese dragon tattooed on his left arm when he was in Hong Kong. He also brought some beautiful china home with him. He and his shipmates also bought some lovely wicker work, which after a while was found to be full of insects and they were all made to throw it into the sea. We gave the lovely china to Pam, who put it in a china cabinet, and still has it until this day, which is a long time since the First World War.

But of course we never gave it to her until she was married. Pamela loved her Dad. She had him to herself until Peter was born; like me she hated him having to return to sea. I never forgot the time when we came back from Newcastle, and after Bert's leave was up, and he had to return, Pamela clung to his trouser leg and sobbed, "Don't go back Daddy!" I could see the tears in Bert's eyes. I tried not to let her see that I was upset too, but it was too much for me also, I could not stop the hot tears running down my face. I think she remembered the hole in the side of the ship, and she didn't want him to go. It was the first time she had made so much fuss but she was a little older and used to think about things, and to her way of thinking, the ship was broken. The next morning, he was away very early while she was sleeping.

It would have saved a lot of heartache if we could have seen into the future then and to know that in a few short months he would be taken off the ship and sent to Admiralty House.

Bert would talk about things I knew nothing of. The place called Vospers in Portsmouth, where apparently they were developing sea rescue launches and motor torpedo boats and no one had realized how important this was to become in the future. The Isle of Wight, already having the World War One destroyers, had now moved on to submarines and seaplanes during these interval years.

"Of course, during the First World War," Bert would say, "people thought that the Great War would be the war to end all wars, when Armistice was announced in November."

I suppose Bert knew it was November and had remembered it as it was near his birthday. I remember them reminiscing about the 1939 Aldershot Tattoo. Bert said it was really a show, to say we were prepared for war. We were at that time living in the face of Nazi threat. We ladies did our best to divert to lighter subjects.

When at last the dreaded day came, Bert was off very early before our Pamela was awake. I told her Daddy kissed her hair so as not to wake her and he would be home again soon.

Mum told me she would take Pam to the shops.
"I've so missed her company."
I said I would busy myself with the cleaning while they were gone. Our little home was so empty without Bert.

Mum's George worked at the Arsenal in Woolwich so I had the house to myself for a while, and really wired in to keep myself from thinking.

My brother, Albert, and Vera had also managed to get a house in Dagenham that had become vacant, it was similar to ours. Albert worked hard on it and also made the most beautiful garden for Vera. They loved it. It was mostly roses, and at the far end were fruit trees.

His pear trees surpassed any I have ever tasted, and I enjoyed the fact that they lived a short bus ride from me.

Vera gave birth to a lovely bouncing boy, whom they named Roy. The doctor told Vera and Albert that they must not have any more children as Vera had had rheumatic fever as a child and it would put her in great danger. They were a bit disappointed about this, so their little boy was doubly precious.

Vera used to come over to us often, in the nice weather. She would walk with baby Roy in his pushchair, past the pub called The Cherry Tree, and then across a big park, called Parsloes Park. Vera liked being out in the fresh air. I would visit them often.

When Roy was ten months old and teething, he suddenly went down with bronchitis. He always looked such a healthy little boy, and we were all shocked when he died. Vera and Albert were crushed. But Vera was to defy all the doctors and go on to have a little girl called Rita. Rita was a smiling faced baby, happy as the day was long. The future was to be ten years for Vera with Rita and Albert. The doctor had told Vera she would die young.

The peculiar thing about that day was, I was preparing Bert's dinner when a feeling came over me. I suddenly wanted to see Vera and my brother. I dropped what I was doing and ran and caught the sixty-two bus. I never did this sort of thing when Bert was coming in to dinner.

I got off the bus at Martin's Corner and noticed there was a crowd gathered at one of the stalls, the greengrocer's stall. I kept on going straight to my brother's house, although I did wonder what was going on. There was no answer at their house but the lady next door to Vera came to her door, and I saw she had Rita with her. She said,
"Come in, Albert's gone to meet Vera," but over Rita's head she mouthed that Vera had dropped dead at the greengrocer's stall. I felt as if I had been turned to stone.

This was a cruel tragedy. A year before this, Albert had a promotion in his job, he was made foreman at Spratts in Violet Road, being sent to the main building. Unbeknown to him, a ring was operating, in thieving. By the time he discovered what was going on he realized he couldn't do anything about it, and it was soon discovered, with him taking the blame. We had been celebrating for him shortly before this.

He was sent to the Isle of Wight open prison for a year.

My poor brother. Of all people, he was as honest as the day is long, and this was all going on long before he was the scapegoat. My poor mother, who fretted for Albert, died after he had been there for eight months. Albert was let home for her funeral and blamed himself. He didn't smile for a long time after that.

When he did come home, his little girl Rita was told he had been away working and was very happy that that job was finished.

Rita asked her dad what his next job would be and he said decorating the house for Mum. They bought the paint and started straight away on the kitchen for Vera.

Vera had been saying the paint was getting on her chest but really it had been her life coming to an end. The forced separation had been hard for Albert and after only three brief weeks, his heart was broken.

Going back to the war years, I heard from Bert to say that he was well; it was lovely to hear from him and at least I knew he was somewhere. He had been at sea for about four years of the war when he was taken off the ship with a couple of others, and had to report to Chatham. Bert was completely puzzled and asked an officer if he knew the reason.

Bert was told that he was probably going to a shore base to train new recruits, at the Gunnery School.

When Bert went before the Chief Officer, he said to him,
"Morgan, you are going to Admiralty House."

Bert opened his mouth to say something when the officer standing beside him kicked his foot, so Bert saluted and said, "Yes sir", then marched out with the officers.

Once outside, the officer said to him, "Morgan, are you mad? Do you want to be spitting your lungs up on a parade ground with a lot of raw recruits? You are going to Admiralty House on the admiral's staff, and you'll get to crew the admiral's barge."

To say the least, Bert was glad. He was instructed to report to Admiralty House in one week and to take that week as leave. Glad though he was, it didn't stop him thinking about the many mates he left behind on the *Arethusa*. Bert said they were a good bunch and had been through a lot together.

That following week for us was one of the happiest before he duly reported for duty. Bert was explained his duties and what would be expected of him, introduced to the other staff and told he would have every third weekend off. This was music to our ears and Bert was to tell me later just how impressive the 'House' was.

Admiral Sir John Tovy, Commander in Chief of the Nor, was in residence at Admiralty House with his wife Lady Tovy, and my Bert was part of their staff.

I set about waiting patiently for Bert's first weekend leave. The three weeks soon passed and I was in a state of anticipation to hear all about it, but I was in for a bit of a surprise. When Bert came home that Saturday he said I was to pack our things and go back with him on Sunday.

It appeared he had to have lodgings in the vicinity of his work and one of his sailor friends had helped him to do this. His friend was lodging in a bungalow in Maidstone Road in Kent and a few bungalows away from him was a place for us, and we soon settled in.

I hastily filled Mum and George in before leaving, and said how lucky we were. George said Bert had done his stint at sea, and after all, he only had a year to do on naval reserve when he was called up.

He must have been nearly forty years old. He had done four years at sea and now deserved a shore job. I said I was only too glad to be able to live normally, whatever normal was now, and to be man and wife and family together.

I asked George if he would mind paying the rent now that he and Mum had the house to themselves for a while and he agreed. It was about thirteen shillings and sixpence (in old money). The rent would be a pound a week for the bungalow in Kent.

So Mum said:
"You're off again then?"

I said as it didn't really seem all that far away, that we would visit on Bert's weekends off, or at least some of them.

Mother was pleased she might be seeing us a bit more often than she had first thought. I had a swift clean of the house (including the porch and brass knocker) and told Mum not to get down on her poor old knees. It wouldn't get dirty with just the two of them, and I would be home soon.

We journeyed to Woolwich, then across the Woolwich ferry. Across the other side we caught the bus to Gillingham in Kent. When we finally arrived at our destination, we walked through a pleasant avenue of trees to Maidstone Road.

On the corner there was a shop whose sign read, "We sell everything", and someone had written between the words "nearly". Three bungalows down from the shop was the one Bert had rented, and he had the key, so he quickly opened the door and let us in.

It was so different from living in a house, and not going upstairs to bed. It was an extremely nice double fronted bungalow, but only part of it was for us – the two big rooms on the front.

Bert then introduced us to Mrs Jean Pendelton and her two children, Robert, eleven and Trudy, eight. It was nice to know

Pamela would have some company. Mr Pendleton was away in the army.

Kent was a lovely county and we eagerly explored at weekends. The cherry orchards, plums and apples were a beautiful sight to behold. Masses of deliciously smelling blossoms everywhere. So far removed from the war, or so it seemed. We shopped in Gillingham, and one thing that surprised us both were the amount of cars for sale. Bert reckoned that their owners were either abroad or perhaps among the missing. If we could only have afforded one. We would have had a very cheap car. There was a problem though: petrol coupons were practically unobtainable.

The garden at the bungalow was big and had apple trees and large juicy Victoria plums, and this year looked as if it was going to be a bumper harvest. Bert would often turn up with bags of cherries he'd bought on the roadside on his way home. We would all sit in the garden, with red stained lips. Oh blissful times, despite everything.

Pam was four and I sincerely hoped the war would be over before she was five. I was beginning to get anxious about her schooling.

Although she had books, and I read stories to her and nursery rhymes which she knew off by heart, she was beginning to know small words.

In the bungalow, I noticed there was a machine (a treadle one). I didn't know if it was Jean's. Well, if anything was going to make me feel at home it was a sewing machine.

I trundled away on it when Pam was asleep. First, I made Jean's two children a pair of pyjamas each, and a few other little jobs, including the mending. I felt quite content.

When Bert would come home from work, he would ask me how my day had been. I'd done some sewing, and taken Pam to the corner shop. Nothing very exciting, but dying to hear about anything to do with Admiralty House.

Bert told me the dining room was huge and sumptuous. Sir John would sit at one end of a very long table and Lady Tovy at the other, to eat their meals. Bert and I would laugh at things like trying to pass the salt. It was nice to laugh. There wasn't much to laugh about during those awful war years, but I was forever grateful my Bert was on dry land.

He followed every aspect of the war, on sea, land and air, and tried hard to find out about his ship, the *Arethusa*.

Bert also described the Minstrel gallery, and in a corner of the long room, a small band played every mealtime. One of his jobs was to iron Sir John's billiard table.

There was to be a ball at Admiralty House. Bert came home full of excitement one day with an invitation for us. This was to be a very big occasion and we all looked forward to it. For myself, it was very exciting as I was going to see inside Admiralty House myself, instead of just hearing about it from Bert, even if it was only the ballroom perhaps.

When the day came, it was raining, and when we made our way there, I remember I had a red umbrella. A couple of women walking behind us commented on my 'sunshade'. It seemed cheerful colours for the rain hadn't reached Chatham.

As we arrived at the imposing entrance, a uniformed member of staff welcomed us in. It was so grand and made us feel very important.

The ladies were shown straight away to the Queen's bedroom, and this was just to be relieved of our coats. I was more than impressed. It was so beautiful that I know I stood for several minutes trying to take it in. As you walked, each step just sank into the carpet. A dressing table, bigger than anything I had ever seen was very ornate, as was its stool, and there were, so it seemed, acres of wardrobes.

At the large windows were richly draped curtains. I couldn't really take it all in in those few short minutes I was in there, I suppose it was more of an impression. We tidied our hair, repaired our make up, then we ladies swept down the grand staircase to the ballroom itself. On our way down, we had a view of the large fireplace and fire blazing away in it. There was music playing softly and it was all very wonderful.

We mingled with the other guests, were introduced, and stood about talking in little groups for a while. Then the band began to play dance music and couples began to dance.

All the different uniformed men looked really smart and the ladies' dresses, long, short, flowing, tight, and so colourful, began to mass on the floor. When a waltz was played Bert asked me to dance and I floated around in a dream.

During the evening I was asked to dance by the Flag Lieutenant. I was quite flattered. He seemed all gold braid and tassels and was a good dancer. I don't think I trod on his toes or he on mine.

The ball ended all too quickly for me, and I know Bert enjoyed it really. That's usually the way when you are having a good time. We were soon putting on our coats in that lovely room and wending our way home again.

Later, Bert made a reference to 'Flags'.
"He was all done up like a carnival horse." This was so unlike Bert.

He was too much of a gentleman to ever say anything out of place, and I thought secretly that I detected a little bit of green, so I told him all about the Queen's bedroom.

All too soon we were reminded there was a war on, and during one of his duties at Admiralty House, dealing with some papers, Bert learnt that his ship, the *Arethusa*, had been hit badly with the loss of over half the crew. All his mates he had known and fought alongside were also gone.

Bert was sad for a long time. He took it very badly and for a while the only way to describe him was bereft. I can feel for him still now. His safe shore job was no consolation although he was forty-three (the year was 1943), as I remember.

It was a far cry from the year 1916 when Bert first joined up at the age of sixteen. I think the only war that Bert knew of at that tender age was the battle of Jutland. I remember at some time Bert saying to someone that the outcome of that battle that was fought at sea was never really known.

Even now, I can hear him saying that Germany never really believed we would go to war. It's been about three hundred years since war was actually fought on the soil of Great Britain.

Last year had seen the invasion of the beaches of Dieppe and Lord Mountbatten saying we were going to stop the enemy.

Now, the Normandy landings. The long awaited second front. Bert told me that our troop ships were steaming across the Atlantic, a lot of them packed with Americans. I knew Bob Hope was entertaining the troops, and a friend who had been in London said you could see every known uniform there.

On the wireless, General Montgomery was saying things like, "The tide has turned and we are beating the enemy," then we would hear 'worker's playtime'. I always enjoyed hearing this.

In fact we heard all sorts of things. There was a pipeline being laid underwater to France to carry fuel for our army, and they were joking that, with the weight of our fighting might, it was only the barrage balloons keeping our island afloat... it made us smile. Also, the talk was of the preparation of the launching of the 'life line' Mulberry Harbour. This was thought a crazy idea by a lot of people.

And they said so. But nevertheless, take our own harbour to the war we did. I remember seeing pictures of it. Great floating concrete jetties, being towed across the water; crazy idea indeed, but it worked and was a miracle in my eyes, even to be attempted.

I remember something that didn't work. Bert explained how the stretch of water before you could land on the beach to fight the enemy had been cruelly booby trapped with miles of submerged iron ribcages of giant proportions, and to make it worse, millions of mines, in order to scupper our landings.

Apparently a rolling device of giant wheels would go before and let the men know where the bombs were and the underwater objects. But this wasn't successful as I recall. I don't remember what this was called.

I do remember the famous 'Swiss Roll' and the ingenious invention called the 'Carpet Layer' for landing tanks. I couldn't believe my own eyes when I saw pictures of our tanks and armoured vehicles rolling along this man-made contraption. Some things really stick in your mind.

Like being told our fighting power on the Normandy beaches was four thousand troopships and over one thousand escort warships. I write these words but it is still incomprehensible to me. I try to imagine now those scenes.

That summer I enjoyed the luxury of picking tomatoes, lettuce and lovely juicy Victoria plums and decided to take some home to Mum that weekend. She was always glad to see us. Pam was always saying, are we going to see Nanny, or when will we be seeing Aunt Rosie? I think she liked being in her own home, and I liked to catch up on the news. Before I left I would strip the beds and Jean would take the washing. This helped me and I paid Jean a few shillings which she was glad of.

As the summer wore on, Jean one day asked me if I would like to go hop picking with her. I was a bit doubtful, and didn't really think it was my scene, but Jean explained that a lorry called for the workers and everyone was friendly. So I decided to give it a go.

The following week I went along with all the others. A burly rosy-faced man tossed my Pam up into the lorry to a pair of waiting arms to her squeals of delight. This became a ritual for all the children, while we climbed up as ladylike as possible. We introduced ourselves to each other and the day progressed with an air of jollity about it.

As we passed under railway arches we all sang and shouted loudly, to hear the echo. Pam soon caught on and loved it. I said to Jean,
"You will have to show me what to do."
She answered, "It's easy, you'll see."

Hop picking was easy and I don't know what I was worrying about. Of course, Pam tried to pull a few hops off, but soon got tired of that and amused herself along with the other children. The whole crowd of us got on very well and the time just flew round. I worked alongside a friendly person who was a policeman's wife, she was very nice and had twin girls, six years old.

Jean mentioned I was a dressmaker, and she asked if I would make her daughters a coat each. I said it would be after the hop picking was finished, and she agreed, as they were to be winter coats.

Most mornings were misty to start off with, then turned out very nice. The others said this was real hop picking weather. Someone always produced hop picking apples for the children, big juicy bright green ones, and they would all sit on the grass munching away and chattering.

On a couple of occasions, Bert turned up to lend a hand. He thoroughly enjoyed the experience. Being out in the fresh air and sunshine amongst a happy atmosphere. I became quite expert at picking and earned myself a few extra shillings. I will always think fondly of the Kent countryside and my hop picking days.

It was time for me to make the little coats, and with the material, lining and buttons bought, they were soon cut out, machined, and ready for a fitting. The policeman's wife brought them round and we were all pleased with the finished result. Soon, Bert would have to lodge in the barracks, which he wasn't really looking forward to, and so I mentioned to Jean that I would soon be returning home to Dagenham. Jean told me she was disappointed, but she knew I would be glad to see more of my sister and her family again and Mum and George. Bert would get home every third weekend. He said it might even be oftener and I said, "That's good."

The following weekend I packed our things and we said our good-byes. I reflected, as I watched the Kent countryside roll by, that Bert wasn't really all that happy with us returning home. Things were hotting up again and I knew Mum and George were now using the shelter a lot again.

Once again I was in my own little house. Mum hopped about delightedly and hugged Pam.
"Oh Flo, I am so glad to see you." I was glad to be home and hoped it hadn't been a mistake. I was soon back in the old routine, and still not knowing whether I was wasting my time, but things had to go on.

I went round the corner to see Rose and we hugged. She told me Mum had been with her often while George was at work and was still very nervous.

"I am glad that she had you close Rose, I knew you would look out for her while I was with Bert." We chatted away like two squirrels and caught up with events in our separated world. We were happy now and said we would take what came (happy that is in the sense we were a unit together in this mess).

Life seemed to resume the old pattern: the air raids, the dug-out, the clearing up, and the vegetable garden. Doing our bit whenever the opportunity arose, and helping other poor unfortunates to get straight. We shared whatever bits and pieces we had and we survived remarkably well. The ration books were a bit of a bind but I was able to do some swapping of liver for eggs and such like, most of my bartering done while queuing for my potato ration. They were quite meagre rations as I recall, and there were four of us. How some poor devils managed I do not know.

Rose told me there were quite a few bombed out houses around her, and that Jeff had been very upset when helping to get people out of the rubble. He had found a baby buried by bricks and carefully uncovered it as the baby didn't seem to have any visible injuries, and he was hoping... but it turned out to have no head.

"Flo, he came home and stood staring at our baby in the cot, then cried in my arms."

I told Rose about Bert, and the way he discovered the news about his old ship.

"Rose, you know I'm sure Bert thinks he should have been with them. I thank God for his shore job, but I know it doesn't rest easy with him. Although he's only once ever given a hint. He said to me one day, 'Flo, what the hell am I doing piddling about on the Admiral's barge playing sailors?'" Unlike Bert, he would spend long periods in quiet thought.

Rose and I agreed that troubles shared were troubles halved, and we laughed and cried together. This dammed war. When we were down we would sing, 'Rule Britannia', we always felt better after that song, and we weren't ever going to be slaves, it was 'Do or Die'.

I had not been home many weeks from Kent when I was informed by the authorities that we would be evacuated again. The war was intensifying and we were definitely in a target area, but Liverpool... None of us wanted to go. Rose and I could not believe Liverpool was a safe place to be with our children.

Mother was anxious to pack us off, but nothing was going to budge her. Both Bert and Jeff thought the authorities knew what they were doing. Bert said to me, "I really think you ought to, Flo."

So, a few days later, we found ourselves in Liverpool. We still didn't believe it was a safe place, and were all apprehensive. This time we were very fortunate with our evacuation lodgings. It was in a pleasant place with a nice big bedroom. I was so relieved to know we wouldn't have to live cramped. I wasn't complaining, but it did make life easier to have room to move around, and not have someone else's belongings piled around you.

The speed at which the authorities had moved us out was borne out by the almost immediate battering Dagenham and the Dagenham docks, the Thames and main roads, took.

Rose and I agonised over Mum, but she always sounded cheerful. It was a very nice woman who owned our lodgings, with her two daughters. Her name was Mrs Jones and her eldest daughter had been in hospital.

She asked me if I minded her girl having the top of the milk to help build her up. I looked at my healthy, rosy, bouncing Pam, still tanned from the summer in Kent, and agreed readily. Rose was in lodgings just around the corner, so it felt a bit like home from home. It turned out that her Jeff's two sisters were also lodging close by, so we felt like one big family.

We had been there a few weeks when Bert and Jeff managed to get down to see us together. We were really delighted and all feasted hungrily on the tomatoes and plums and bags of fruit they brought. Bert was loaded down and it was fun sharing it all out.

Bert took us across the river on the ferry, so I can claim to have been across the Mersey. Bert and Jeff managed to stay for the weekend and this time it was nice to know we had enough room for them.

They went, promising that if it was at all possible, they would try and be with us again. I suddenly did not mind being evacuated, as I didn't feel cut off any more. The men did manage one more such visit. This time Bert took us to New Brighton and we enjoyed being a family for a few hours.

By this time things were getting pretty bad all round, and I told Bert that Rose and I were seriously thinking of going home. Shortly after this we packed our cases, said our good-byes and were once again on our way home to our little houses in Dagenham to take our chances along with the rest, but not before Mrs Jones and her daughters had begged a story from Bert of his experiences in the Navy.

As always, Bert never really talked about events at hand, but related something from his twelve years after the First World War. As I recall it, he was somewhere up the Yangtze River in China. In that part of the world at night the night sky was a really wondrous sight with the stars much bigger than here. Bert was such an interesting man to listen to, so his storytelling held a circle of big eyes and interested faces.

It appears they had anchored for the night and he and some sailors were on deck admiring the night sky as they waited to take over the watch. During the night they were boarded by pirates. These were roughneck, opportunist killers, the real cut throat knife in the teeth job, barefoot and silent. It would only be a matter of minutes before most of the crew would have been killed in their hammocks.

But the watch were alert and used split-second initiative as swift action was needed. Swift action they got. The handful of sailors on watch turned the ship's steam hoses on them, with a hundred per cent success.

The outcome was that the government of that country was so impressed with our Navy that they managed to enlist our help. It appeared that marauding gangs had been terrorising and killing and looting, but they had been difficult to track. Bert's ship was used to flush out these gangs, a puzzle at first. Then they discovered they lived on islands and were coming in at night, then disappearing back on the islands. When Bert was relating the story, we all had goose pimples, and there was quite a bit of oohing and aahing – they loved it.

As soon as we were back home we experienced the Blitz. I cannot put an exact time to it, but I remember wondering if this was the end. It was so bad, could we take any more? The people's morale was very low. I remember walking a few yards down my road and turning to stand and look directly down Cannonsleigh Road towards the Thames. Billows of smoke and fire filled the sky to a terrific height. Both sides of the river were alight, all the warehouses.

As far as you could see, there was nothing but flames. At night, it was frightening. Surrounded by an orange glow which would take some putting out.

But tomorrow was another day, and the British were a hardy lot. They weren't called the Bulldog breed for nothing and the evidence was all around me.

From my little house I saw the Battle of Britain fought. An expanse of sky over Hornchurch Aerodrome, where I could see the fighting, fought by so few for so many.

Many of the enemy planes were intercepted as they came in. A lot reached the Aerodrome to try to knock out our Spitfires.

Many a pitched battle I watched along with the neighbours, our hearts in our mouths. (And we were supposed to be in the dug-outs.) A sudden nose-dive and stream of smoke, and a shout would go up, trying to gauge whether it was theirs or ours.

There was no doubt about the bravery and skill of the men in their flying machines. The tight circling, ducking and weaving, climbing and diving to miss the blasts of white fire on their tails, only to go full circle and be the ones doing the chasing.

I am reminded of the afternoon I was shopping, and was standing with some other shoppers watching an aeroplane making a stream of smoke and getting lower and lower in the sky. We saw the pilot bale out and come to land very close to the shopping area. We all started running to that spot.

He spoke in a foreign language and nobody understood. He was getting a battering and some of the women ran into the butcher's shop to get the knives. They were going to set about him. I stood watching, numb, thinking, this man might have dropped a bomb on my Bert's ship and he might be floating dead somewhere right now.

The shopkeepers restrained the women and someone discovered he was Polish, and on our side. Poor devil. I walked home feeling sick and confused. This is a terrible war.

All this happened while Bert was still at sea. There was a lot of trouble over this incident, which was natural, and the authorities wanted to make sure it never happened again.

When I had arrived home from Liverpool, Mum told me my brother Albert over near the Cherry Tree had taken a direct hit from an incendiary bomb. I went over there.

There was an enormous hole in the roof of his and Vera's house. A small crater in the path to the front door. When you opened the door you looked down a big hole in the floor through the boards and footings into the earth. I could clearly see the bomb device in the bottom. There were more holes at the back of the house and up the garden. His lovely garden. It was ruined. They received a new carpet for the lounge.

The incendiary bomb seemed to be a cluster of stick type bombs, and to this day we will never know why the ones that fell on Albert and Vera's house never went off. The men came and removed them, and the children around found it exciting and just another story to tell at school (when they were able to get there).

May the seventh was my birthday. Bert had managed to arrange to be home for that weekend. During that weekend I jokingly asked him if he was going to buy me a present. He said, with a twinkle in his eye, "You've had your birthday present."

I replied, "I have not."

"Yes you have, don't you remember last night?" Then he ran up the stairs laughing.

I said, "That's not fair." He did give me some money later to buy a little treat.

As it happened, this turned out to be a wonderful present. I was again pregnant. Later on when Bert came home on leave, I told him. He said, "Are you sure, Flo?"

I said, "I'm as sure as your tea and kipper are making me feel sick, but I will see the doctor."

When I did see the doctor he said that as I didn't have any problems with my first he didn't think I would have any with this one. I knew he was right. Pamela was now five, I couldn't help thinking that I would be thirty-two by the time this baby was born and Bert nearly forty-four. But I was happy, so what.

From the newspapers, it looked as though we had all but annihilated the enemy planes. But, they were to come up with the V Bomber and the dreaded Doodlebug, before they had finished with us. When you heard them come over, and the engine stop over the top of you, you knew it was coming down there and then and your number was on it.

There was a lot of dashing to shelters now, during shopping, that's if there was one near by.

We were hearing of Montgomery's victory in the desert, and news was sounding better these days. We were still losing ships to the U-Boats, but on the whole we were cheered up.

Bert had told me how Paris had fallen in about 1940 without a shot being fired, but now they were starting to uprise. There was talk of big plans afoot, we now know they were for the big D-Day landings which finally took place in June. It all depended on the weather; for days it was on, then off, but finally embarkation took place on the sixth of June. The weather had been really bad, with storms at sea. Just what you didn't want for landing men on beaches.

It was still only the end of January and my time was near, so as I only had two weeks to go, I thought it was time to pack a bag. That same night I left in a hurry and my little boy was born at midday on the twenty-first. My delivery sister kept me guessing when I asked her what my baby's sex was. She paused then said, "What have you already got at home?" I said a little girl. There was another pause, then she said, "Well you've got one of each now, it's a little boy."

Those few minutes of suspense had been awful, but I forgave her her little joke. When she handed him to me I looked to see if he really did have his 'belly lanyard' as Bert was to call it later. He weighed six pounds and three ounces. Three ounces heavier than Pamela.

Mum sent a telegram to Bert straight away. To our surprise he came home almost at once. Pam ran to meet him, shouting that she had a baby brother.

Bert's dialogue was the same as before:
"He's a little rabbit." His face looking at us both spoke volumes, and for a few seconds the war disappeared. Bert had to return the next morning to Admiralty House, but when he got there he was sent for by Lady Tovy.
"Morgan, you never told me your wife was expecting."
I'm sure Bert could not imagine himself saying, "Lady Tovy, my wife is expecting a baby."

Lady Tovy told him to go with her. Evidently there were sacks of clothes and toys for distribution for times like this. She also gave him two nice white towels, and some soft white nappies.
"A little wooden train for your little boy and a small doll for Pamela."

Bert was very grateful, they were lovely things. That was not all. Lady Tovy told him, "Morgan, you are to have a fortnight's leave, I will see that you get a pass."

Bert came straight in to see me, all smiles. He whispered to me later, "I don't know who's running things at Admiralty House, Flo, but I'm not complaining."

While I was in hospital having my baby, there was plenty of noise going on; the guns in Parsloes Park were banging away - we called it the 'bath bun' for some reason, it sounded like banging on an old tin bath. There were other gun emplacements around, the noise was frightening. A hospital sister came and said, "I am afraid the bomb-proof ward is full, will you mind going into a side ward, you can keep your baby with you." I agreed and was put into a side ward; well, if anything was going to happen to me it made sense to have him with me.

I had knitted a lovely pink dress scalloped round the bottom, and a nice shell pattern, and I wasn't going to be able to use it for my little boy, I exchanged it for a little blue dress with a woman who had made the same mistake that I had. The blue dress was not as elaborate as the pink one but that did not matter. She was thrilled with it and said, "Are you sure?" I assured her I was.

When asked what name I was going to give him, I said Peter. If Pamela had been a boy we had chosen the name Peter so now we had a Peter – a pigeon pair, as they say.

The family came to fetch me home. We had ordered a taxi but it never turned up, perhaps it was because I had ordered it too far in advance. Bert wanted to order another but I did not want to hang about. It wasn't far to the bus stop so that's what we did, after telling Bert I was perfectly all right. So Mother, Bert, Pamela, myself and baby travelled home on the bus. Pamela kept wanting to look at him, so did the other passengers on the bus.

I was glad to get indoors, it was pretty cold. Peter didn't have an elaborate boat pram like Pam had. Things were hard to come by during the War. His Aunties knitted him some things which all helped. Pamela had a doll's cot in which we put another pillow and placed Peter. He fitted in nicely. The only thing was, Pamela thought she had another doll, but it was very useful to pop into the dug-out quickly.

Our council house was called a maisonette. It consisted of two bedrooms, a bathroom and toilet upstairs, a living room and kitchen downstairs, so we now had to think of living space. It was all right at first with just Pamela and myself in one room and Mum and George in the other bedroom when Bert was away at sea most of the time, but now things were a little crowded.

So Mother and myself started going more often to Green Lane's rents offices to try and get another place to live, as we were now overcrowded. All we could get out of them was they would have to go back to Stepney, and try to get a place back where they had come from originally. I told them Mother only lived there three years, and was bombed out twice, and that she had been with me longer than three years. I could understand the awful job they had trying to place people, but it didn't stop us from keeping on trying.

Mother was to live with me seven years in all. In the end she got a flat in Stepney, with two flights of stairs. I was very worried for her, but she had to take what was on offer. But that wasn't until a couple of years after the war. We realized they were not going to get anything in Dagenham. Pamela was to be six on the twenty-second of April. There were nearly six years between her and Peter.

We had a party for her, and invited all her cousins round. Because her birthday was late April she could not start school until after the August holidays, so she had been at school nearly eight months by the time she was six and loved it. She was an outgoing little girl, and always on the go. My friend Mary's daughter said it would be a good idea to start her at dancing school to use up some of her energy, and that she would take her.

Pamela could not wait to get started, so I entered her for ballet, tap and acro. She went twice a week, calling for her friend Patricia who was eight years her senior.

Things went on much the same the last year of the war, Bert getting home every third weekend. The worst that could happen was to have a Doodlebug fall on you. Although there were near misses, we were fairly lucky, and kept our fingers crossed at strange noises.

There was summer to look forward to, and lighter evenings once more. The enemy were sending missiles instead of planes; this could mean that they were short of aircraft. We sincerely hoped so although we were always on tenterhooks.

But the war was coming to an end, it was plain to deduce from the way things quietened down.

And as Bert was one of the first in, he was one of the first out. Churchill was a long time announcing it was over; I expect he was being careful and didn't want to jump the gun, as the saying goes.

The men coming home were fitted out with a suit, raincoat and hat and shoes; well, after six years the moths had fed off their old clothes. I remember Bert was very pleased with the shoes, they were a good make, we could not have afforded that make ourselves.

The chap in the stores said to him, "What size do you take? Bert said a six. "A six? That's not a foot!" Bert said, "What size do you take then?" "A nine," he replied. Bert said, "That's not feet, that's plates of meat!"

When Bert told me this, I laughed to think he had got his old camaraderie back, and laughter was easier to come by again.

He also said that there were loads of spivs waiting outside the barracks to buy the clothes off them, they had been packed in a square cardboard box, but the clothes were worth much more than the six pounds they offered.

The first thing he did when he arrived home was to try them on to see what I thought about them; I told him he had made a good choice, so we were both pleased.

After a couple of days, he thought he had better go and see about his old job. He duly arrived at his old place in Stratford Marshall Taplows, where he was greeted by some of his old workmates; he was sad to learn that some had been killed in the bombing and others had not returned from war.

Now everyone was able to get on with arranging their Peace Parties. We went around collecting whatever people could afford for what was to be the day of days, and counting the children, and collecting the bunting, and checking who could lend kitchen tables, and ordering paper cups and paper plates. When the great day came, it was not long before the bunting was up; a long row of tables appeared down the middle of the street, and tablecloths were placed on them. The children were very excited: it was hard not to fall over them.

Next out came the cakes and jellies, and plates of all kinds of sandwiches – all the Mums had really turned out tops.

Games were arranged for after tea, and prizes for the fastest runners. The men had it all in hand, and it all went smoothly. My friend Mary was down one end, keeping the children amused, while other Mums were all along the backs of the chairs, helping the little ones. During the races the sweets began to run out, I think there had been too many winners, so we cut the liquorice boot laces in half, and I found a bag of gob stoppers that I had put aside because I did not want the little ones to have them. There was loads of food left over, which we shared among the families.

I must say Bert was in his element – he loved children – and in re-acquainting himself with his neighbours and some of their children that he had never seen, he was really enjoying himself.

I looked at his happy face, and felt that he was really home at last. All he said was, "I only hope that the other tea parties were as good as ours."

The weeks following the war, you would see little groups of people discussing what was happening, such as the Russians reaching Belsen and other German camps and freeing the prisoners. There was always someone who knew a person that was imprisoned, like I knew Eddy and Alf, and as people walked by they usually joined the group, and it was lovely to see all the happy smiling faces with something to smile about at last. We knew there were a lot of very sad people too, and we commiserated with them, but joy was uppermost after all the anxious times – a great black cloud had been lifted.

We were thankful for all the different forces that had fought with us, to help us to be victorious: without them we would not have made it.

It was lovely to see all the different men coming home, or going home to their own homes.

People could hardly believe the horrors of the concentration camps. German townspeople denied any knowledge of them, but so awful were the conditions you could smell it for miles; you could not have not known. Those poor people.

We heard that Hitler was dead. There were so many rumours, but he was supposedly killed in a bunker, when all was lost.

One of my favourite pieces of music was the Warsaw Concerto. The composer had stood on a hillside looking down at his beloved Warsaw lying at his feet in ruins, thus the words at the beginning,
'And here I stand, the dust of Warsaw at my feet.'
It must have been so sad, I think about it every time I hear it played; there was nothing left standing. Other countries suffered the same fate. This time I hope that it never happens again, it is something we must make sure of, or at least the coming generations must.

About a year after the war was over, Bert used to sit with me in the evenings and discuss some of the happenings. He was fascinated with D-day and some of the things that it entailed, like the Mulberry Harbour that was built in this country and taken to Normandy, and the sections joined up to allow our tanks and lorries to land men and supplies. Also the fuel pipeline that stretched across the sea to keep tanks and lorries moving, and the wonderful Army doing their job under dreadful conditions.

Our friend Eddy was taken prisoner in North Africa, and taken to Italy, and from there was marched to Germany, and was imprisoned in Stalag Thirteen for the duration of the rest of the war. His wife Ivy had a little boy but Eddy didn't see him until after the war.

Looking back when Bert was on duty at Admiralty House, crewing the Admiral's Barge or accompanying the Admiral when he visited the barracks, Bert said when they knew he was coming they rushed around in a panic, to make sure everything was shipshape. It was laughable really because back at Admiralty House, his wife would say, "Henry, stop whistling in the House", or, "Henry come here", and Henry would obey; a very different Henry to the one on the parade ground.

It's a good job his men could not see him!

The First Officer also had to obey her: Lady Tovy would say to him, "Take these eggs back and tell them I want all brown ones." Bert said he had to sit beside him and try to keep a straight face. Bert did not get any of these jobs and I think this was because he was an older man.

I said to Bert, "She should have had a wren to help her."

Bert would say to me, "Flo, you would make excuses for the Devil himself!"

Bert said on the lighter side, when things were quiet, Admiral Tovy would order the barge and slip across to Calais and fetch a couple of cases of champagne for himself and his friends; that was a plus for the Admiral.

The governor at Marshall Taplows told Bert there was a job for him. Bert asked what the wages were now. The boss said three pounds eight shillings. Bert was stunned: his wages before the war were three pounds, two shillings and six pence; he could not believe that they had hardly gone up after six years of war.

Bert said, "We cannot live on that."
The boss said, "That's the worst of you chaps coming back, you want the earth."
Bert said, "What's the matter with that, and if that's the best you can offer, you can keep it."

It was hard work before the war. In the cold weather, his hands would always split at the tops of his fingers through being in cold water. Bert had dry skin, so that was part of the trouble, so perhaps changing his job would be the answer.

Later that week he went after a job on the buses.

When he came home he said he was going to be a bus conductor. "Is that right?" I said.
"Straight up," he said. "I got the job."
"Oh good," I said.
"Not that good," said Bert, "I will have to work most weekends, as you only get one Sunday off in seven. I will give it a try, I can bike it to the bus garage, so no fares, that's a point in its favour."

The next day he went to Chiswick to start his training.

We were better off money-wise than we had been for years, with a little bit of sewing that I could manage in the evenings when the children were in bed besides.

Bert raked his old bike out of the shed and proceeded to give it a good clean; it was in fairly good condition, as he had cleaned it from time to time, although it was pretty old.

His first bus was the eighty seven, a very busy route. I asked how he had got on after his first day. "All right I think." "I will ask you after you have done a couple of weeks," I laughed.

Bert settled into being a bus conductor very quickly.

We soon got used to early and late shifts. He was full of little happenings on his bus; when you are dealing with the public, you are in the thick of life, especially when you have spent years at sea, and life is once more on an even keel.

Sundays off were few, but we made the most of them when they did come around. Weather permitting, we always went out with the children. When not visiting relations, to whom we owed promised visits, we went to Barking Park, a favourite venue of ours, as long as we were out in the fresh air, although we sometimes took them to an afternoon matinee at the pictures.

We had a very nice garden, two-thirds of it was lawn so the children had plenty of room to play, but Bert's idea was to get me out; he thought I needed a change, which I never argued with.

Pamela's Daddy had promised her that when he came home from the war he would take us all away for a nice holiday, so she kept asking him about this. He told her that when Peter could walk, that is when we would go.

Peter took his first steps on his first birthday in January, so his Daddy was able to tell Pamela that we would be going away that summer, so we started looking at addresses in Bognor where there would be nice sands for the children to play on. We settled on July, and promptly wrote away to a couple of places; we had an answer from both.

The lodging that looked quite near the beach we accepted and wrote back sending a pound deposit, as required.

This was in March, and July seemed a long way off, but nice to look forward to.

July duly arrived. We set off for the coach that was to take us to Bognor; we were having two weeks, and were very happy at the prospect.

We found the lodging easily. We climbed two flights of stairs, and there was our little room. Two single beds had been pushed together and there was a pot under the bed.

Can you imagine the four of us in those single beds, Bert and I trying to balance on the edges?

Evidently the room belonged to two young girl lodgers that had to be shifted into a spare room that was bunged up with all kinds of rubbish. How they managed I don't know.

Anyway, no cup of tea was forthcoming. Bert said let's hurry up and go out, so we dumped everything and did just that.

The children were hungry, we had only booked bed and breakfast, so we had decided to eat out. There were plenty of food shops along the front, so there were plenty of choices to be had, and people were friendly, so food wasn't any problem, and prices were reasonable; beans on toast was a teatime favourite, fish and chips was another at lunch time, or any time special for us. I always had a supply of rusks, and there was always fresh milk to be had for Peter, and he loved chips. We managed all right. Breakfast at the guest house was nothing to write home about, especially when she served up a kipper for a one-and-a-half year old child. The landlady had wrapped a bit of sacking around one of the table legs and said, "Put the boy there", which was silly. I would not have sat him near the table leg. I said to Bert, the blessed table is not half as good as our mahogany table with the Queen Anne legs at home. He just said that I must not be so touchy about things.

For most of those two weeks it rained, so we went to plenty of shows, but the two Thursdays were dry, which was very lucky as my mother came down for the day, and it was lovely and sunny. She could not believe we had all that rain, so we spent every nice day on the beach.

The following Thursday was just as nice, when Bert's Mum and Dad joined us for the day.
"We ordered fine weather," Bert's Mum jokingly said, so we sat out and enjoyed it.
"How have you managed?" Pop said.
"It hasn't stopped the children, they were quite happy to put on their macs and get on with it."
"Good," said Pop.

But I did not tell either of the parents about our little accident on Bognor front. It was fascinating to watch the waves lashing against the sea wall, with the seaweed rolling back and forth. Suddenly Peter toppled over and landed on the seaweed below. It was about a six feet drop, I went to jump down after him. Someone grabbed me and said, "Leave it to the men, missus!" as the sea was very rough that day. He was not hurt, thank goodness. A kind lady gave him a banana and he soon stopped crying.

Bert and another man had run down a groyne and picked him up, and another man had to lie down on the promenade to reach for him as they handed him up. That shook me up for the rest of the day. I thanked the chap who had helped Bert, they both were wet but made light of it.

From that day I have never liked heights. I, who had sat on top of Logan Rock, had lost my nerve.

A year later at Ramsgate I could not go near the harbour; what a different holiday that was.

When we arrived home from Bognor, I went to use my ration books, and the tea coupons, bacon coupons, and soap coupons were cut out for the month. I had a shock! We were there for the first two weeks in July; taking my soap was like adding insult to injury as I had taken my own soap, but Bert said let it go – we won't make that mistake again.

My sister Rose was quite indignant. She said you should not let her get away with it. Rose and Mum helped me out with the rations; that woman had interfered with three people's rations: mine, my sister's, and my mum's, was the way Rose looked at it, and she was right.

Rose had another baby boy whom they named Roy. That made three boys, so she found it difficult to have a holiday; her eldest boy was only a couple of months older than Pamela.

Pam was still going to the Kitty Harris Dance School with Patricia her friend, and loved it.

Peter loved his sister and she him; when she came home from school and found him crying, she was concerned because he very seldom cried, but this day he was very upset and was trying to tell her why. We had a couple of chickens, Clara and Jane. Clara was his favourite. Peter had got off his chamber pot to see her when she pecked what she thought was a worm.

It was not so much that he was hurt, but that his Clara had bitten him – he was pointing his finger at the chicken and sobbing. Pamela picked him up and tried to console him, then she put him in his truck and pulled him round the garden; he soon cheered up.

I noticed that Pamela had a love for all animals. She would not even let me tread on an earwig. They gave me the creeps, but she said, "You must not kill them, they make very good mothers, they have a family too somewhere."
"I didn't know that, sorry, dear."

Horses were her best love. When she was a bit older, she spent many hours over at Romford Chase. I spent time on my sewing machine, to give her the money for the bus and her riding lessons, but most times as long as she had the bus fare, that's where she would be.

The year following the Bognor holiday, we were going to Ramsgate. Someone had given Bert an address, saying it wasn't all that near the front, but the food was good. We duly wrote to the address, and received a reply within the week, so that was settled. We had the first week in July, and I had to tell Pam to be patient as she wanted to start packing straight away.

Peter was about two and a half and Pamela eight, nice ages, I thought, to take on holiday and I meant to make the most of it.

The coach duly arrived in Ramsgate, and the children were naturally very excited. They had spotted the nice sands, the sea and the boats. We said, we must find our lodgings first and move in. A taxi was the easiest way to find the location, it didn't seem all that far.

We were welcomed, and the landlady said, "I will bring you a pot of tea – I expect you could do with one."

"That would be lovely," I said. There was a nice double bed, a single bed and a cot.

Bert said, "What a difference from last year."

"Yes, and the weather is good too," I said.

At breakfast the next day, there was a nice crowd of people sitting around individual tables. I was glad to see there was another family with children sitting near us. We had a good breakfast, and then collected our things for the beach. I suppose it took our little party about twenty minutes to get to the front. The beach already looked crowded, but we found two deckchairs and made ourselves comfortable; the children got to work on making sand castles almost at once. Their Dad said, "There's no hurry, we are here for a week." About half an hour afterwards, Bert spotted the couple we saw at breakfast with the two children. They were trying to find deckchairs, so we waved to them, and called them over, introducing ourselves. They were John and Doris Warren, and the children were Jacqueline and Peter. The boy was about one and a half, and the girl was nine. Work started on the sandcastle straight away.

The two men went off to find two more chairs, and left us to get acquainted. Doris said they lived in Welling, Kent. I told her I came from Dagenham. Meanwhile the children were having a whale of a time, lucky to find friends so soon. The men arrived back with two more chairs, so we all made ourselves comfortable.

Dinner was at six thirty, so at five thirty we thought we had better wend our way back. We happened to see the taxi driver who had taken us the day before. "How's things?" he said.

"OK," we replied.

"Pile in," he said.

John said, "There are eight of us."

"Half a crown," he said.

"Yes, please," and off we went, so we booked him for the week.

On Thursday we thought we would do something different so we decided to have a look at Broadstairs. It was very nice, we had our usual ice creams there, I think it cost half a crown for their four ice creams, and the same for ours. John said, "They will have us in the workhouse, Bert."

Doris said, "You should not walk into posh ice cream parlours." Our holiday friendship was to last a lifetime. We had to return on the Friday night, because Bert had to work on the Saturday.

Our new friends saw us onto our coach on Friday afternoon.

"We will miss you," Doris said. "I wish we were going now, things will seem very flat without you all."

"We are going to meet up very soon, so we will look forward to that," I said.

A couple of weeks later, they came to us for the weekend. We all got on very well, it seemed to cement our friendship there and then. We decided to try and spend our next holiday together, which we did.

We took a caravan each at Walton-on-the-Naze, well known for its beautiful sands and pier to enjoy.

Bert was thinking of getting a second hand car, but they were very hard to come by: the war had made a shortage.

My sister's neighbour, who knew a bit about cars, went with Bert to look at one. It was a Ford, and looked like it had been left in the rain for some time. They wanted two hundred and sixty-five pounds for it.

After trying to get the price down, Bert decided to pay up. When I thought of all those lovely cars we had seen in Kent, and now they were practically unobtainable.

We could not complain, that old Ford served us well. The next year eight of us poured in like old times, us and the Warrens, and our luggage, off to Walton-on-the-Naze. We were to have that car nearly fourteen years, with one re-conditioned engine, and finally sold it for one hundred pounds.

Bert was getting dissatisfied with the buses. He used to come home and tell me all the irritations of his day: how one passenger would come dashing up saying, "You're early", and another would say, "You're late".

Bert would say, "You sit next to him, he says I'm early."

Another time Bert said, "What do you think Flo, my driver would not stop for this woman waiting in the rain, with two little children." I said perhaps he got out of bed the wrong side this morning. Bert had been on the buses for four years and wanted to be a driver.

He had a medical, and was told he had a hernia, so could not be a driver.

"I have had enough of being a conductor Flo, so I am going to look for another job," and this he did the following week.

He had heard they were taking on men at Fords, so he biked down to their labour office at the Chequers, Dagenham, and joined the queue. For a while nothing happened, then a door opened and an official came out; pointing to men in the crowd he said, "You, you and you."

A chap standing next to Bert said to him, "You stand more chance it seems to me, if you have your best clothes on." Bert decided to go back the next day in his best.

The following day off he went looking very smart in his best. The crowd seemed to wait a long time before the Ford's official came out. He pointed to about three men, and then at Bert. He was taken into an office – it was his turn to be questioned. He was asked about the Navy, and why he did not return to his old job, and then about the buses.

Bert was forty-five when he left the Navy, and after four years on the buses, this made him forty-nine. He thought he hadn't stood a chance, so when he came home and told me he had a job, I was very glad, and I said, "Is it the janitor's job?"

"No, oiler and greaser."

We both laughed.

Ark Royal escort under bombing attack, HMS Arethusa.

Constantinople, Turkey, November, 1922.

Firing range, Bisley.

Ship's painting party.

First World War, Russian convoy, Baltic.

Attack on Convoy by U-boats.

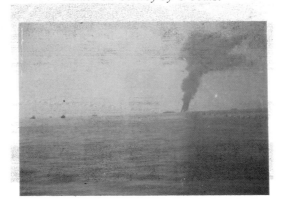

Wash day, dobying, World War Two.

Bert and shipmate on Gibralta, World War Two.

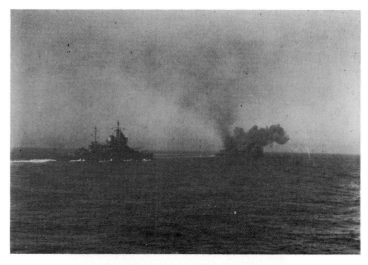

U-boats torpedo strikes home, World War Two.

Aircraft gun deck, HMS Arethusa.

Landing Parties, World War Two.

Exercise abandon ship, HMS Arethusa.

Portrait taken in Valletta, Malta, World War Two.

HMS Verity destroyer, World War Two.

Hermes aircraft carrier Hong Kong.

Hermes aircraft carrier.

Bert's job at Fords was like a whole new era starting for us. We were happy and settled down to enjoy it – such a change to early and late shifts, and working weekends. When I told Rose and Mum they said, "Good". I said, "Very good", and they were both happy for Bert and I. Rose said we ought to celebrate.

"I think perhaps a drink at the Round House" (a public house in our area), which we duly did.

Later that evening we had a sing-song round the piano, with Bert's sister Doll and her husband Sid harmonising. Doll was a good pianist, and we sang some old favourites. One of Bert's was 'My Little Grey Home in the West'. I loved to hear him sing: Bert had what I called a dark brown voice, a sort of a baritone, and it blended very nicely with all the other voices. It was a satisfying day, and I hoped we would have many more.

Bert settled in at Fords. He used to love cycling through the Goresbrook Park in the nice weather. He did this for quite a while until a neighbour a few doors down asked him if he would like to make up a foursome in his car to Fords, to which Bert said yes.

It was very nice to have weekends again. Pamela's school had not liked her being away sometimes, on her dad's rest day, so she would not be told off any more by her headmistress. Peter was soon starting School at Monteagle and Pamela would be going to Bifrons.

My sister Rose had a little girl. She now had three boys and a girl. She called the girl Marie, a girl at last! You can bet we all made much of her, and were in the throes of spoiling her, but we needn't have worried – she turned out trumps. Such a help and a Godsend to her mother. Bert wasn't at Fords very long before he was made a charge hand, which was a step up, and made things easier for me. I didn't need to do so much machining to make a bit extra although I had more time on my hands with Peter at school too. I spent a little more time on the garden. The lawn looked like a bowling green, and I made a little kitchen garden. That Essex soil was very good for growing things, especially roses.

I did eventually go and get some outdoor work; I wasn't one for sitting still, and it nicely filled in the gaps. Another benefit was that Bert did not have to go into the kitchen every time a customer came for a fitting. By the time you had made them a cup of tea, poor Bert had missed the boxing or football that he wanted to watch, so that was an improvement. He had been very patient about my work, but that was over. When I think I used to do as many as five or six weddings in a year, and there was the clearing up to do! I suppose I was cheap; really, having things made to measure should cost more, not less.

Another thing about outdoor work: you did not have to go and get it if you did not want it.

So summer days I went round my sister's or she came round to me, and Mother came to visit more often.

In the nice weather sometimes our sister-in-law came over. Vera would walk across Parsloes Park with her little girl, Rita, and we would spend the day in Rosie's garden.

In my sister's turning, they were getting up a coach trip to Margate; we were looking forward to the event.

Eventually the day dawned bright and sunny. We had a lovely time on the sands. Margate has a beautiful golden beach. I went in the water with the youngsters. We splashed and jumped around, and thoroughly enjoyed ourselves, and then sunned ourselves on the beach.

There's something lovely about seeing children enjoying themselves with the war forgotten and way behind them.

Children grow up so quickly, you feel you must make the most of them while they are still young.

Pamela was soon to be leaving school. Where had the years gone? It was hard to believe she was fifteen, and there wasn't much in the way of jobs.

Her headmistress said she would do well in a shop, and that C & A were asking for school leavers; Pamela said she would give it a try, and they took her on.

The money was very poor: by the time she paid fares to the city and tried to clothe herself there was very little left. The worst time was stocktaking, and not getting home until nine thirty; most evenings it was gone seven before she arrived home anyway.

One day a customer asked Pamela what C & A stood for. Pam said, "Coats and 'ats", which was meant to be a joke, but this humourless lady complained to a supervisor and Pam was sent for and told that she would be placed on Macintoshes for a fortnight. This was used as a reprimand, I suppose, but it did Pam a favour really, as it made her think about changing her job.

So Pam decided to do a typing course at night school, and when she finished, found herself a job in Thames Road, which was a short bus ride away, and much better money.

Pamela was much better all round. She finished at five thirty which pleased her most, and was now able to go to cookery classes with her friends; I was happy to see her not looking so tired all the time.

My sister Rosie's youngest son Roy, became road manager for Brian Poole and the Tremeloes, and gave him the nickname Albert.

That summer the four of us went to Devon. Pamela said, "Let's try a farm for a change", so we looked through the brochures and came up with Bideford, and a place called Swan Farm near Appledore, with a large house standing in large grounds. We made ourselves at home and were allowed to help with turning the hay. Pamela enjoyed collecting the big basket of eggs, although she didn't much like seeing the battery hens: they had both kinds.

The farmer let her help him milk the cows, which pleased her, getting up early in the morning and joining him in the milking sheds.

I was fascinated to see all the cows go into the right stalls. Pamela said, "Didn't you know they could read, Mum?"

"Oh, very funny!"

I took some lovely snaps, one where Pam is holding onto the ring in Daisy's nose:

"Hurry up Mum, she won't stand still forever!"

"Well don't let her go then."

I was feeling very nervous: I had never been that close to a cow before. The snap came out very well. Another I took was of her in her riding breeches – she had been riding.

Afterwards we walked on the front. I had saved some bread to feed the seagulls; Pam was holding a bit up when a seagull took it from her hand.

When I had the film developed at a little shop in Bideford, Mr Littlejohn asked me what camera I was using. When I told him it was an old box Brownie, he was surprised. He said, "They come in here with their expensive cameras and their pictures are not half as good as these."

Bert was very impressed because he had said we probably needed a new camera, but I had said we will have the film developed and if it isn't any good, then we will buy one.

After Mr Littlejohn's comments I bought a couple more films, and went on snapping: one of Pete sitting on the plough, another stroking a pig, or trying to; some we took on the beach at Westwood Ho! where there were miles of beautiful sands. The two children seemed to like it best back at the farm, where we helped or hindered, as was the case, and the farmer's wife brought us out delicious drinks and scones. If it rained during the night we would turn the hay again to allow it to dry, at the same time enjoying the lovely views.

One fine morning at the farm, we decided to go to Westward Ho! for a swim. Bert had gone back for the camera. We waited in the porch for him. When I heard the farmer's voice, he was giving someone a good telling off.

"You've been gone three nights when there is work to do here: get your breakfast and get started."

When the farmer rounded the corner there was the sheepdog following him with his tail between his legs; he knew he had been out of order but we couldn't stop laughing – it was a relief to see it was only the dog getting a telling off. Bert wanted to know what all the laughing was about. The farmer told him about the dog:

"When he goes off, he is away three nights, that's how long he takes to do his courting."

Bert said, "Well, what do you know, randy little beast," and joined in the laughter. We then went on our way to Westward Ho!

A sunny day spent in the sea, and sunning ourselves on the lovely sands, we wended our way back to the farm, arriving refreshed and hungry, to the lovely aroma of dinner. At night when all the children were in bed, all except Pamela, all the guests gathered in the lounge, and there we used to chat about the day's happenings. Sometimes Bert would go off with another chap who had a gun, to shoot rabbits. When they came back we asked if they had shot anything. Bert said he had shot a cigarette packet in the hedge, and the other chap said he had shot a baby rabbit. I knew Bert would not say if he had shot anything, because Pam would blow her top. He forgot to warn the other chap.

Pamela told him he should be ashamed of himself, that poor rabbit could be lying in pain somewhere. Her love for animals caused her a lot of upsets – she actually went outside to see if she could find it.

The farmer and his wife went to bed early, but before they did, they brought a tray of tea and scones saying, "Goodnight each", and then they toddled off to bed.

That was one of the loveliest holidays we had spent until that time.

When it was time to leave Swan Farm the children were sad to be going, they had really had a marvellous time. The farmer said to

Bert, "Your daughter is far better on the farm than a good many youngsters born on a farm."

Bert said, "I am glad she has been useful, I know she has enjoyed every minute."

When we arrived home it looked small after the farm, although I'm always pleased to be back in my own place. There was plenty of colour in the garden, and I always left the house clean, so there was not much to do except to unpack and sort the washing that we had brought home, and that could wait until another day.

So we went to let Rose know we were home, and take them some rock; they wanted to know all about the holiday so we sat and chatted over a cup of tea.

Bert's Mum and Dad had bought a little caravan, only a three-berth, but plenty big enough for them both, so we popped down to see them. They were quite happy there, in Walton-on-the-Naze, and were very fortunate weather-wise, and there was always someone popping down to see them.

A year later Bert's two sisters and their husbands also bought a caravan, a four-berth. It was very nice, and we were able to spend our next holiday in it.

So with the kind permission of Doll and Sid and Ivy and Charlie, the owners, we had a lovely holiday. This time our friends, Doll and John, booked a holiday caravan, a four-berth at Coronation Camp, which turned out to be quite near us, so our two families were able to have a nice time together. We realized that the girls were growing up, and would soon want to go holidaying with their teenage friends, but for the present, we were all together once more.

A couple of years before, Bert's Mum and Dad had shut up their house and gone to live with Ivy and Charles, in Ilford, Essex. They had a nice big house, with three bedrooms, so the reason they bought their little three-berth was so they could go off to Walton and give Ivy and Charles some time on their own, which was a good idea for both parties.

Pamela had given up dancing school a couple of years before when her teacher had gone, and she was able to go horse riding more often. She had done well at dancing: once when she had exams, she got top marks for ballet, getting top marks out of one hundred and fifty other children. She was also good at tap dancing and acrobatics.

Peter loved all sports, especially football and cricket, and swimming was another favourite with him. I often think back to when he was quite small. He was playing in the road with a little friend, they were kicking a stone about, when he blocked it with his foot and it went right through a neighbour's window, so his Dad made him take the money out of his money box. It was two and sixpence for a new window. Luckily they were all small panes, and that is what they cost in those days. Peter thought it was a lot of money – I suppose it was to him – but a lesson had to be taught.

But later he pleased his Dad by getting chosen for the Barking Boy's Football team. He was in goal, and his Dad often went to see him play. Bert was pleased when anyone asked him if that was his boy playing for Barking.

Bert had played football and cricket for Marshall Taplows, Leytonstone, when he was working for them.

Pamela and her friend, Shirley, were planning to go away to a holiday camp the following year. Shirley was keeping company with Pamela's cousin Jethro – we all called him Jeff. They decided on Wales. It was a camp in Llandudno, it was just the girls going, and something to look forward to. Meanwhile they were going to cookery classes. My sister's boys always turned up on cookery night to sample their efforts. Rosie said her boys were gannets, usually there was nothing left by the time they reached home.

When we, that is Bert and I, were sitting alone in the evenings, I would try to get him to talk about the war and what happened to him. He was very reluctant, he would sooner forget it, but sometimes I would persuade him to open up.

He began: There was this very dark night, when *H M S Arethusa* silently crept up this Norwegian fjord. Their task was to knock out a German gun. This they did, but it was harder getting out than it was getting in, and I think he said, it was an Italian plane that fired a rocket at them. He said he was lucky, and that some shrapnel just missed his eye, and hit him on the forehead and eyebrow. When he was on leave a couple of weeks later they were little wounds almost healed, and he just said, "It's nothing". I remembered when it happened, but I didn't remind him, as I didn't want to stop the flow of conversation once he had started.

He then said that on another occasion, they were to land supplies for some troops and hide them in a little forest that was near the shore. A sailor pal said to him, "Morgan, you have a little girl, you had better have this." He pulled a little fur rabbit from under his jumper, and gave it to Bert; it was on a tube with a little bulb that you pressed, and the rabbit jumped along. Bert could see it was a very good toy, and said,
"Are you sure?"
He answered, "Yes mate," and scrambled away. Suddenly the whole place was lit up, firebombs were being dropped and the petrol was catching alight. Bert said he was one of the lucky ones, he managed to get back to the boats, to take them back to the ship and away.

The outcome of this was that he never saw his shipmate again so Bert was determined to get that little toy home to Pamela as his shipmate had wished, and he often wondered if his mate had had a feeling he wasn't going to make it; sad but true.

Another time, Bert was telling me of a convoy to Malta. It was quite a large convoy, and they had a dreadful time trying to protect it.
When they arrived in Malta, they only had three ships left of the convoy which was terrible, having also lost some naval vessels. Bert said that he could not bear to think of all those men, guns and provisions lying at the bottom of the sea.
Malta had had a very hard time, being bombarded mercilessly, so they named her The George Cross Island.

Bert said, "Flo, don't let's talk about the Second World War. I would rather tell you about some of the places I visited after the first war, when I was finishing my twelve years' service."

He began: "When we were lying off Ceylon at one time, we were invited ashore by this tea planter to see his plantations. After walking around his private gardens, the flowers, the bushes and the trees were a lovely change after looking at so much water. We then sat on the balconies sipping delicious teas, admiring the beautiful scenery, the beauty beyond description. Flo, if there was ever a place I would like to see again, it was there."

Another time, he said: "We put into Gibraltar Harbour and visited the Rock, and there we saw the famous Barbary apes – friendly little chaps. On the Rock were some large gates, and when they were open at certain times, you could cross over into Spain. We visited all the famous places in Gibraltar: our time was well spent."

Bert also said: "When I first joined the Navy, we wore sun hats to keep the sun off. They had large brims turned up at the edge." I thought he was pulling my leg, but it was true – he found an old snapshot of himself wearing one.

I was looking forward to more of Bert's stories: after all, he had been round the world with the Royal Navy three times.

Bert's mother Caroline, died that winter; we think they may have stayed too long in their caravan: they did not come home until late October, which was a little too long, but Ivy cared for her very well with her Sister Doll helping. Her age was against her, she was seventy-nine.

Pop sold the caravan, and gave us all fifty pounds each; he said he did not want the money.

Caroline had a very nice grave, with a white surround and green chippings, and a white marble open book.

Pop lived with his daughter Ivy, and we took turns to look after him when Ivy and Charlie went on holidays, or to stay with friends, so it worked all right.

I now worked in Ilford. I had done outdoor work for these people, and they kept asking me to work in the factory, which I did. They were a nice bunch of girls, it was good having them to laugh and talk with, and Bert did not mind – he said, "Whatever makes you happy".

We were looking out of the window during lunch break one day, when a girl named Jessie said at those lads over there, see who they are. These boys were going into the police station Which was opposite, "They are the Rolling Stones". I said I had never heard of them, most of the other girls hadn't either, so it shows how long ago that must have been because they became very famous soon after.

When I was leaving, Jessie wrote a lovely poem, all about going to Devon to live. The firm had it printed and put on a card, I still have it.

One day I was talking to a workmate about holidays, and told her that Bert didn't want to go to the sea this year, he preferred the country.
She said, "I think you would like where we went last year. I will bring you in the brochure." I thanked her, and she brought it in the next day. I took it home to Bert who studied it, and then said it looked a very nice place. I agree Bert, a very nice place indeed.

Bert lost no time in booking. I was able to tell my workmate that we had received a reply. On checking our holiday dates, we found we would be there on their second week, who said, "That's nice, we will see you there then".

Ivy, my work mate, and her husband Eddy, became our very good friends. Pamela and Shirley's holiday was booked for August, ours was early July. Peter was coming with us, so the talk was about what to wear and what to leave out as we always seemed to take too much, but we had plenty of time to sort that out. Around that time, Bert had a phone call at work to say that his brother had died, so he rushed down to Laindon to find out what had happened. He had died of meningitis, a shock to all of us. He was only fourteen months older than Bert.

Bill and Nell's family consisted of four boys and one girl. The eldest son and daughter were married, and the three other boys were out to work.

A week after the funeral when Bert popped down to see how they were getting on, Nell told him that she had been trying to get the garage where Bill had bought the car to buy it back. It had been only six weeks before, but they wanted to drop the price such a lot that she didn't know what to do. Bert said, "Well, if I give you a lump sum, and then ten pounds a month, could you manage?"

Nell said, "That would be lovely, Bert, are you sure?"

Bert said he was, and that's better than letting that thieving garage have it.

It was a Vauxhall Wyvern, a lovely car, metallic green in colour. He went down the following week and fetched it home – that's when he sold our old Ford.

Bert and I had some nice outings with Fords. We went to some West End shows and New Year's Eve parties in the West End of London, at the Aldwych, and afterwards went to a brasserie for dinner, and places like that, but I cannot remember the names now though they were very nice times. We also went on outings with the place where I worked. We saw *West Side Story*, and *South Pacific* among others.

We were looking forward to summer once again. Pamela was getting excited about her trip to Wales. Her friend Shirley and she were also talking about Barking Carnival, and going in for the competition for Carnival Queen. They said it would be a laugh, so they put their names down, as it was after their holidays and something else to look forward to.

When Pamela and Shirley arrived at Llandudno, they were very disappointed with their chalet. The sink was bunged up with cigarette ends, the place was dirty, and the beds didn't look all that clean, so they decided not to unpack and to go and complain. The authorities said they could not give them another chalet as they were booked solid, but would send someone to clean it.

The camp did send someone to clean the chalet, but, peak season or not, it should have been cleaned. Although off to a bad start, they did manage to enjoy themselves, and they liked Wales very much indeed.

A few days after their return, Shirley came out in chicken pox. We wondered if Pamela would also get it but she didn't. Shirley had to drop out of the Carnival competition but Pam said she might as well stay in it. It would be an experience.

Bert pulled her leg about it: "You won't win, bet you five shillings you won't."

Pamela said, "I stand the same chance as the others."

I set to and made her a long dress. When she came home from the Town Hall, after the judging competition, Pam told us she was in the finals. Her Dad said, "You are kidding?"
"I am not, it will be in the local tomorrow."
"Right," said Bert, "if you win, I will make it a pound."
"I'll keep you to that," said Pam.

I found myself altering her dress to make it look different. There wasn't time to make her another, even if I could have afforded it; of course Pamela wanted a new dress for the ball, but I said money doesn't grow on trees, and with that she had to be satisfied.
The night of the ball arrived. Pamela set off looking very nice. Her Dad took her in the car – it was the only way for Pamela to be on time. She was a last minute person, always rushing, never giving herself enough time. This was the only thing her Dad grumbled at her about, being such a good timekeeper himself. Bert said Pam would be home very late, so we watched a bit of telly, and then went up to bed.

We were woken by Pamela, shouting, "Dad you owe me a pound!"

We couldn't believe it, because Pam liked her little joke, but she was wearing a blue sash, and a crown on her head. She sat on the bed and told us all about it: she had evidently had a good time. Dad said,

"We'll get to bed now as it's very late and tell us more fully tomorrow", but we did not find it so easy to get back to sleep.

Pamela had a very good Carnival year with the Mayor's car at the door, plus the Mayoress, to take Pamela off to many different functions. When Pam rode in the Carnival with her two ladies-in-waiting, it was a very proud moment for us.

Derek Bond, the film star, crowned Pamela in Barking Park on the bandstand; we have some lovely pictures of the events.

We were invited to the dinner at the Town Hall, with all the dignitaries, plus Derek Bond. We had a little conversation with him, he said he had been very busy that morning, mowing his lawn. Pamela seemed to think he should have a gardener and a swimming pool, but not in those days evidently!

On the Saturday of Carnival Week, there was always a big fair in Barking Park when half the takings went to charity. Pamela was given a lovely bone china tea set trimmed with twenty-two carat gold, of which she still has some.

Derek Bond was given a magnum of champagne, which someone stole off him, but with a big fair on, it was a job to trace. He shrugged it off, but I must say that although Barking wasn't a bad place, we felt that was a black mark against it.

Pamela thought it a great joke getting marriage proposals. There was a smartly turned chap who kept bothering her, and wanting her to go out with him, and one or two others. When she came home from work, her Dad used to say, how many have you fended off today?
"They all want to get in on the act," Pamela would reply.

Pam only liked one boy, his name was Ronnie. He acted as her protector, I think, although she was not serious about anyone at that time. I encouraged her to invite her friends in. She had a nice friend a few doors down named Maureen who had won a scholarship, but didn't see as much of her as Maureen was at college. One day Ronnie and another boy came in. I realized that he was shy, hence the other boy to back him up.

At Christmas we had Bert's Dad to stay, to let Ivy and Charlie spend the holiday with their friends. We took him round to Rose and Jeff's on Christmas afternoon, and he proved to be very entertaining. He sang some old songs that we had heard before, but they hadn't.

One was 'To Be A Farmer's Boy', another was about a chap who 'went to the bottom of the sea and it wasn't a dozen farthings deep, and they just took him off to the graveyard, just wiped a tear from their eye and they just blew the bob that they gave them for the job, and they would see him in the sweet by and by' – these are a few of the words I can remember. Considering Pop was very old, he still sang a good song; he had us laughing all over the holiday, though he was almost ninety.

How Pop remembered all the words to the 'farmer boy' song and then twisted them all about when he did all his jobs wrong. We all said we wouldn't get it right, it would be worse than a tongue twister to us – we know because we tried it. We kept Pop with us for two weeks, and then returned him to his daughter where we spent a pleasant afternoon, swapping Christmas stories, and we were glad to hear they had had a good time too.

During the next couple of months, Pamela and her friends all seemed to be pairing off. Pam and Ronnie, Shirley and Jeff, and so on. They met up sometimes in a group and all went out together.

Pamela still had her year of office to complete as Carnival Queen, and was called on for different occasions; it was all very interesting, though she seemed to take it in her stride.

Peter spent a lot of time over at a place called Matchstick Island. I don't know why it was called by that name, it was down the bottom of our turning, and was a lake with little sail boats on it. He used to help the man who looked after the boats, and was quite happy to do so; if you wanted Peter, you knew where to go and find him, he wasn't far away.

When Pamela was eighteen, we bought her a record player and let her choose a couple of records, so we dispensed with our old gramophone; it had done us good service but we had to wind it up for each record. It was a nice piece of furniture, it stood about four and a half feet high and had a lovely top to it. It was mahogany and would have made a nice coffee table and it had two small doors in the middle which opened out to let the sound out. One of my nephews asked if he could have it, and I let him take it; it seemed funny without it, but the space was welcome. We had a piano, we bought it before we had the children. I remember we went into East Ham to buy a chicken, and came back with a piano. Bert loved to tell our friends that tale, or to anyone who said, "Oh I see you have a piano!"

We had a lady come each week to give Pamela lessons when she was about eight years old and she used to say:
"Pamela you haven't been practising."

Well, this lady moved to Clacton, so I said, "I expect you have driven her away", and as Pamela didn't seem too keen I didn't bother anymore.

But in later years she could knock a tune out by ear. But many a sing-song we had when Bert's brother Bill was alive, and Bill junior played the piano accordion. My friend Mary from next door but one, her husband Harry said he knew a tune in Spanish. Mary said he's not getting away with that again. We passed round word around that we were going to put a stop to Harry's fooling, so we let him start, then everyone joined in the fun with every foreign word we could think of, it was hilarious. Harry put his hands up and said, "OK you win" but he did lead us in some old well loved tunes.

We all had a good laugh – I do not think you can beat a piano at a party for entertainment.

One of Pam's friends would pop in at times and give us a tune, I always enjoyed hearing it played. I used to play it at times when I was alone, and not if anyone was listening. I was fond of good music, so I would not foist my playing on anyone.

I was to learn many years after the war how my Bert really felt about being on convoy.

I was given a brief insight into his true feelings, and the harsh reality of how it was for the young men of that time.

In 1980, our daughter Pamela was attending a class called 'Writing for pleasure' at the local college evening class when the subject for her homework was, "The Sea". Pamela asked Bert, her Dad, if he would put a few brief lines down for her about his feelings when at sea as a young man, and she would build a story around it for her homework, and these are the original words he wrote in his own hand:

'A bitterly cold morning with a strong blustery wind blowing from the north, bringing sleet and whipping up the waves of an already rough sea.

With the glass still falling, the hardiest of sailors must fear for the hours ahead, when the weather would get much worse.

Looking along the deck of the ship from aft to fore there did not appear a lot to see: boats secured for sea, barley rafts lashed to the superstructure amidships, the bridge and ladder, twin upper deck torpedo tubes trained outboard ready for action if required.

Every now and again a wave would crack inboard sending a rush of water along the steel deck of this naval destroyer and finally down the scuppers to return from whence it came.

No sign of life was visible except some movement on the bridge: possibly the officer of the watch, a signalman or look-out.

The watch on deck were there all right and at their posts of duty, but this being the starboard and weather side, were taking advantage of whatever little shelter they could get from the elements.

As a young seaman, feeling very lonely, homesick and I suppose rather bitter at being where I was, 'doing my bit' as it was called in a war that was to end all wars to me was a senseless slaughter of human lives for the sake of power.

My thoughts were of the warm and cosy home and loving family left behind in London. Were they safe? How were they standing up to the constant bombing of the town? Surely this war could not go on much longer, a few more days or perhaps even tomorrow it could all be over – wishful thinking of course but somehow it seemed to help keep one's spirits up.

My thoughts were suddenly brought to an end by two short shrill blasts on the ship's siren and repeated at intervals, shattering the silence, a sure warning to ships of the convoy and other escort vessels that enemy submarines were in the vicinity. An immediate burst of speed, the ship heading over in reply to the wheel being put hard over to take evasive action against any torpedoes that may have already been fired.

Action stations having been sounded on the ship's claxons, the ship is an efficient fighting force in seconds of the alarm. Depth charges are exploding as destroyers guarding the convoy pinpoint what may be an enemy U-boat.

After about an hour or so with nothing surfacing or reports of any ship being hit or sunk, the order is given to stand down and we return to normal patrol as before, assuming that, if an attack had been made, it had failed or it could have been a false alarm.

I am back again with my thoughts – how long before the next alarm? Or, how many times before we reach our destination? With the weather rapidly worsening with huge waves smashing into the very slow moving cargo boats and tramp steamers, we with the other escorts having to keep circling them and keep our own speed down, this nightmare journey seems never-ending. One consolation as my thoughts ramble on, is that no enemy submarines could possibly attack in such weather. How wrong I was proved to be before the end of the day, but that's another story.'

Pamela wrote a story around these pages, and the outcome was her tutor shedding a few tears, saying, "Don't mind me, Pam, I lost a young brother at sea. He was only nineteen, it was a U-boat's direct hit on his ship and I have just realized what he must have gone through."

Pamela's story ended with this elderly gentleman staring out to sea with the wind blowing through his greying hair, a black box in his hand. It was April and his son's birthday. He opened the box, and the sun glinted on it for a moment. This was all he had left of his son, and Pam called it, 'April Son'.

Pamela asked her Dad if she could go with Ronnie's brother and wife, and Ronnie, to Jersey for their holidays. Bert said, "If it is all right with your mother." It was OK with me, so they later came round to make plans for the said holiday.

We had to face the fact that she was nearly nineteen, and we had to trust her; it was the first time she was to go off with a boy on holiday.

We made arrangements to go to Exmouth and take Pop with us; we wanted to take one of Pete's friends as company for Peter, but they were all going their different ways. Peter was now thirteen and a half, and we knew he would soon make some friends – he usually did.

The following day he was asked to join a cricket match. He played with this group of children most days, there were girls and boys, and seemed a very nice bunch. When Pam and Ron came home from Jersey, they had a surprise for us: they had become engaged while in Jersey.

Pamela said,
"Is it all right, Dad?"
"Of course it is a surprise but why in Jersey? Did you think we would object?"
"We bought the ring in Jersey because you get better value for your money."

Well, that seemed a good enough reason to me, and it was a very nice ring. We invited Ron's people around. He had one brother, Sid, and one sister, Jean. His Mum and Dad were just like ourselves, and we got on all right. So we had a very convivial evening.

Pamela's friends asked her when she was likely to get married, and she told them that they had some saving to do first – perhaps eighteen months' time, or thereabouts. So Pam and Ron started economising straight away. I said to Bert, "They are very keen to save. We must also prepare for this coming wedding."
He replied, "There's plenty of time."
I said, "Time has a way of creeping up on you, I must have a talk with her about bridesmaids and so on."

Pamela told us she would like to get a job in Barking Town Hall if she could. Through being in the Carnival she had become used to going in and out, and liked what she saw. So she asked around and found there was a job to be had, as secretary to the road safety officer. After applying, she found she was lucky enough to get the job.

Her Dad and I were pleased; it was good to see her trying to better herself. Pam started her new job there and then. Ronnie who worked at Fisons, where his dad was foreman, said he would also like to get another job as unloading ships was very hard work, so he was going to keep his eyes and ears open.

He later went after a job in Fords, and was lucky, as it was better money, so they were both serious about saving we were glad to see.

While Pam went to cookery classes, Ronnie was a physical instructor at Bifrons evening classes, so they were both well occupied. Although Ron was not the big and beefy type, he was incredibly strong, as he has proved many times. As Peter was coming into his fifteenth year, Bert asked him what kind of job he was thinking of going in for.

Although Peter's birthday was January the twenty first, he could not leave until Easter. Pete mentioned lorry driving. Bert said, "You would have to be older and have a licence, and you don't want to end up lorry driving, and any way, I will teach you to drive when the time comes. Meanwhile you had better think about a trade."

A few days later his Dad asked him if he had come up with anything. Peter said, "I think I will try and get a gas fitting job."

Now he had made up his mind, he was impatient to leave and get started working and earn himself a bit of money, but the time went quickly round and the day came when he presented himself at the gas company offices at last.

Peter told his teacher at school, when asked about his job prospects, that he was trying to get a gas fitting job. His teacher said very good, I hope you are successful. We were glad to see that Peter lost no time presenting himself at the gas offices. They questioned him and told him he would have to do four years' apprenticeship; this sounded a long time to Peter, but said he would give it a go. He was also told he would have to do one day a week at East Ham College, so each Monday he went to college. Peter had a nice bicycle that he had bought himself out of his paper round money, so when he was sent out on gas jobs with his fitter he could put his bag of tools on his bike. You could have your tools stolen in those days too, if you did not keep your eyes on them, which often happened.

Pete learned a lot from his fitter, and looked forward to the day when he would be sent out on his own – that day would come eventually; it was good that he liked the job, that's half the battle.

When he had been at work a year, he bought a second hand motor bike and proceeded to do it up, and made a good job of it. He loved tinkering about with machines, like most boys do. He kept it in the shed. The only thing that was a nuisance was that he had to wheel it through the hall, and I dared him to touch the walls or dirty the wall paper, as we had recently refurbished the hall and kitchen.

One day to my horror I came home from work to find him spraying the bike in the kitchen. Oh no, I said. There was this fine black spray all over the new walls we had done in the kitchen, on the new paint of the cupboard and back door, and on the new gas fridge I had bought, from which they had allowed me ten pounds off as Pete was an employee. It was covered in fine black spots.

"Why did you do it in the kitchen?"

"It was too windy out there, Mum."

I just sat on a chair and wept. My lovely kitchen was spoilt. When he saw how upset I was he said, "I will get it all off, Mum."

I dreaded to think what his father would say when he came in.

When Bert came home, he was angry with Pete.

"What a fool thing to do, haven't you any more sense than that? Every paint spot in this kitchen has to be removed, and you are not going out until you have done it."

Well that job took Peter a week, I know, because I helped him, that is, whenever Bert wasn't around. It was back-breaking, arm-aching stuff; I must admit I felt sorry for him, but as his Dad said, it was through thoughtlessness, and he must learn to think. Pamela gave him a little pep talk, she said:

"You know Dad is sprucing the house up, getting ready for my wedding, and don't forget you are my best man." As Pam went, she called out to him, "No more silly tricks!"

I was glad to hear the last of that episode, and started concentrating on the dresses for the wedding. I wondered if Pam had decided on the bridesmaids, and how many. I knew she was looking at material and asked would I go with her to choose. I needed to know how many bridesmaids and the sizes, then we could make a start. We later went into a huddle about the family, we chose three cousins, who were all around ten years old, and two of Pam's friends – five in all.

The first suitable Saturday morning we were off to Petticoat Lane. We had a good rake around the stalls and shops. In one of the shops we saw some lovely lace, after holding it this way and that, Pam decided she liked it very much, so we bought the lining to go with the lace too. The gentleman said what about bridesmaids.

"Yes, we are looking for suitable material."

He proceeded to show us some samples, and we actually found it hard to choose they were so lovely, but we also had to think about the price. Pam settled for a pretty embossed material, a very pale pink, with a white raised flower all over. We made for home, well pleased with our purchases. I thought I would return later to the same shop for my own dress. There was excitement when the girls knew we had bought the material, and they all clamoured to see it, and June the sixth could not come quickly enough for the younger bridesmaids.

For the next six weeks there was a lot of coming and going for the bridesmaids, but the fittings were all going well; I left Pamela's dress until last.

When I had finished the younger one's dresses, I had made them long with a full skirt. Pamela's two friends' dresses were calf length – that is what they wished them to be – but I wasn't prepared for the younger bridesmaids to wish that theirs be calf length too! Pam said she wanted everyone to be happy, and would it be too much work to shorten them, and that she would help. I said, "No problem," and proceeded to cut the bottoms off the three dresses. It was a lot of extra work, as they were very full skirts, but I eventually managed. Then I made a start on Pam's. I loved seeing the lace take shape: a fitted bra bodice, a slash neckline, fishtail cuff sleeves, a full skirt, ground length. At the back was an insertion of fine net frills, and the waistline was folded over these so that the frills peeped out from the fold; it was Pam's idea and she was finally satisfied.

Bert had taken Peter with him into Barking to be measured for a suit, and as both fittings were ready, he asked me to go along with them, which I did. Bert said jokingly, "If only you could have made suits, we would not have this bother."

I said, fancy saying a new suit is a bother! I sometimes made his trousers, but jackets – no way.

Their suits were very nice, they both had navy and looked smart. My dress was in the process of being finished. It was beige with a pretty pattern, and I had a large hat to match. After getting everyone's approval, I was satisfied.

A friend of ours was a school caretaker of Thames School, Barking, and had told us that the school hall was a good place for the wedding reception, so we booked it, some months before, so that was all right. The cake was ordered along with the flowers for Pamela and the bridesmaids. The cake was three tiers, with a tiny bride and groom on top, and there were baskets of real flowers for the bridesmaids; the scent was lovely.

Replies to the invitations were coming in, and lists were being made as to where people would sit, and the cards were then printed to make it easy for people to find their places at table.

Two wedding cars were booked, as there were dozens of relatives with cars offering to help, but two would be ample.

The wedding was to take place in St Thomas More's Catholic Church, Dagenham. We had to explain where this was to a lot of the guests. Bert's sister Ivy and her husband Charles had to come from Norfolk, his sister Doll and her husband Sid from Hainault, his other sister Violet and husband Harold came from Rayleigh along with their daughter Marian, who was one of the bridesmaids. When all five bridesmaids were assembled, they went into one of the bedrooms. Pamela's two friends, who were the elder bridesmaids, said they would get them all ready which was a great help, so Pamela and I had a bedroom to ourselves.

Downstairs, Bert and Charles were organising drinks, and someone was making welcome cups of tea. Ivy brought me one – her smile said she knew that was just what I could do with.

Pamela had me on tenterhooks as she was late coming back from the hairdressers. Saying, "Don't get in a tizzy Mum", she began to dress. I could then relax, and get myself ready.

Peter called up the stairs:
"Cars are here, Mum."

I hoped he was going to do his best man bit all right; once he had got used to the idea, he seemed to throw himself into the job.

I don't know how Pamela felt, I just found myself in church, hardly knowing how I got there. All weddings are lovely. The bride, the groom, all the guests, the colours, the flowers, the scents. I was in a kind of euphoria, and gave myself up to enjoying it all. It was the culmination of all that hard work, and well worth it. It was a long time to Peter's wedding, but this was here and now, and at last I could relax. I suppose most parents felt like I did, well at least I hoped they did.

The register was signed, and we were following the bride and groom outside for photographs, and looking through the album is a nostalgic feeling, remembering, lovely to look back upon.

Lots of photographs were taken at St Thomas More's Church in Barking of Pamela's wedding.

When the photographers were satisfied, everyone was sorted into cars and were off to Thames School for the reception.

There was lots of laughing and joking, the sort of repartee that goes on after most weddings. We eventually went inside where lots of little tables were set up with half a dozen chairs around each. The meal was very satisfactory, and Bert thanked the caterers. Peter read out the telegrams, some were rude, so I won't dwell on those. Bert made a speech which was cheered and friends added bits to it that had us all laughing. Friend Eddy's band played for the dancing; it was very satisfying to see everyone enjoying themselves. We gave Pam and Ron a good send off. They were honeymooning on the Isle of Wight. It was June and they had good weather.

They became lodgers in the upper half of a friend's house in Romford, they made it very comfortable and we went to visit often. Barking Council asked Pam to hostess the girls for the Carnival Competition; also the Barking Photographic Society asked Pam to sit for them as she was photogenic.

At seventeen, Peter became engaged to Diana; he also passed his driving test the first time, so a double event was celebrated. After a few months Ron and Pam decided to buy a house in Barking, a very nice location near Barking Park. They made some alterations to it, in fact I worried what they would do next: an archway in the hall, a pile of rubble in the hall, a chimney breast taken down, another pile of rubble, but I did like the patio. Pam said to Ron, "We're all right, Ron, Mum likes something." Bert just walked around smiling. He said to me, "You worry too much." I expect he was right, but I breathed a sigh of relief when it was all done.

Bert went with Peter to see the apprentices' passing out exam in Fulham. They had to fit a gas heater, and appliances. He passed, so he became a gas fitter and plumber.

We helped him buy a little seven hundred weight van from Fords for his tools, and to make things a little easier on jobs. Bert's sister Ivy became ill, and was to be away eight months, so we took Bert's Dad, Bill to live with us; he was a lovely old chap and no trouble at all.

At this time Bert's hernia was proving troublesome. Fords got Bert into hospital quickly, where he was operated on and made a quick recovery. We went to visit him. There was snow and ice on the ground; icicles were actually hanging from the car. It was the Vauxhall, Bert's car, and Ronnie drove. We were advised not to be out on the roads unless it was absolutely necessary.

Although Bert said we were not to come, he was pleased to see us.

The next time we visited him, it smelled like an ale bar. The men were all sitting round a big fire, drinking Guinness, which was evidently doing them good.

A couple of weeks after Bert was home, a chap visited him from Fords and said he should stay home a bit longer   after all, it was a double rupture – but Bert was itching to get back to work; I told him he would not get a putty medal for rushing back.

Pam and Ron bought a collie dog. We had never had a dog, only all cats, so we were all interested in this lovely dog. Come the summer, we all opted for Devon again, and seeing our friends were going, we naturally wanted to join them. Bert asked Pam and Ron if they would like to join us. Ron said, "No Dad, we will be all right": they had spent a lot of money on the house. I told Pam that Dad was disappointed as he wanted Ron to drive to save him the strain. Ron said, "That's a different kettle of fish, Dad, of course I will drive."

We set the holiday up and were all set to go. Peter and Diana were off to Yarmouth with friends, and us, with Fable the dog, off to Devon.

We had a very good holiday with Pam and Ron, who became very friendly with the owners. Pamela told them that she would like to run a small hotel, and the upshot of talking was that if they sold their house and went to work for them for a year, they would teach them how to run it, then they could pay them so much down a year to buy it from them. This they did and were soon off to Devon with their furniture, the dog Fable and their black cat; we had mixed feelings about it at the time, but their minds were made up.

Their first year was a bumper year, everyone wanted to go and see them, and this we all did at different times.

Haldon House was a lovely place in a lovely setting on Haldon Moor, and had twenty-two bedrooms, and was twenty minutes from the sea, but the country and the moor were beautiful and a lot of people just sat around and enjoyed the beautiful views; you could see Woodbury Common in the distance.

That year Peter and Diana were getting married in August but it looked like being a very busy time for Pam and Ron and they could not be spared to go to the wedding. Ron said he would not go, if only Pam could be spared to go, as he was her only brother.

Pamela was very upset, she so wanted to go to her brother's wedding. She said some people just did not understand about families, but the owners said no, they were too busy.

Diana's wedding reception was to be held at a hall in Barking – I have forgotten the name but it was next to a police station. They were married in a church built by Wills, the cigarette people. It was situated at the bottom of Cannonsleigh Road, a very nice church. Once again I made the wedding outfits; Di's wedding dress, and two bridesmaids, one was her cousin and one her friend.

I have wedding albums of both Peter's and Pam's weddings, lovely to look back on. Back at the hall it was good to see all the relatives. We were looking forward to the pleasure of hearing Eddy's band again. As it was Bert's sister, Ivy's, and Charlie's wedding anniversary, Bert had the band play the Anniversary Waltz; we left them dancing a long while before joining them on the dance floor.

Peter and Diana spent their honeymoon at Haldon House where Pam and Ron made them very welcome.

While staying in Devon they looked round for a house, and found some nice places being built in a village called Stoke Cannon. We were surprised and pleased for them.

Bert asked Peter what about his job with the gas company. Peter said it would be all right.

I think Bert was worrying more than Peter about his job. He told Pete to take the car the next weekend and stay with his sister and go to the gas company, and find out about his job. Peter did as his Dad said the very next weekend. Bert could not rest until they came home. Pete said that everything was all right as long as he had his GCE, which he did. The honeymooners were staying with Di's parents for a while and were going to Devon in November to wait for their house to become ready in January.

Pete's Dad and Di's Dad had to sign for the property, because they were both under twenty-one. Di's Dad said jokingly, "You had both better behave, or the house is ours."

Peter got taken on with the Exeter Gas Company with no trouble at all. Bert said, "That leaves us Flo, we will spend our holiday looking for a place in Devon." Our friends Ivy and Ed said they were going to do the same.

One day during our fortnight's holiday at the beach hut at Teignmouth that we used to book each year, we were on our way for our usual swim when we saw some bungalows being built down a very steep slope; at that time they looked very intimidating. Lower down there was a valley, with two houses right at the bottom, and a farm. After debating about having to go and have a look, we decided to do just that.

We drove down to a little hut and a man said he would show us what was on offer. There were about three finished bungalows, and we were pleasantly surprised: big windows with lovely views. A twenty foot lounge, two double bedrooms, a large kitchen, fair sized bathroom and a toilet.

Ivy, that is Eddy's Ivy, looked at me and said, "I would like number thirty-eight", and as the bungalows were the same, I settled for number forty. The house agent went outside and said to our husbands, these two are sold. I must say they looked disappointed.

Bert said, "Well done."

After signing the contracts, the agent said, "Would you like to come for a drink?" We said yes – after all, he had just sold two bungalows!

Bert was saying when we get home, we must see about selling our beach hut at Walton-on-the-Naze, also our shed, the flavel debonair gas fire, and several other things would have to go. I had not got that far, so I said, hold on Bert, let's finish our holiday first.

Pam and Ron had been married six years when they were expecting their first baby in November; they had a little baby girl and they called her Angela. Bert got a long weekend off so we went dashing down to Devon to see our first grandchild; she was lovely, like a little cream doll.

Our bungalow would be ready in January: we would be able to help with the baby – we could not get there quickly enough. It would be just a year after Peter and Diana had moved. Our little family would all be living in Devon, although Pam and Ron had a Spanish couple, Rossie and Umberto, also a couple from the village. Students in the high season, cousins when on holidays; twenty-two bedrooms is a lot to manage and they were glad of any help. Haldon House had a big games room, a full size billiards table, a good floor for dancing, a bar, a large fireplace at one end of the lounge, a big square oil heater the other end, several armchairs, and a piano – very cosy. When a crowd of our friends were staying, there was usually a couple of piano players among them. In the evening someone would start playing the piano. It was all right at first, nice and soothing – the guests would be reading, but after a while the music would change to songs like Cigarettes and Whisky, and songs of that calibre; you could not help laughing at the antics, and people would come out from behind their books and join in. Happy days.

In the winter months, Haldon House did weddings. Friday night was Moose Night, Wednesday was Country and Western. Occasionally, there were car rallies, needing beans, egg, bacon, tomatoes, bread and butter for early morning appetites.

Bert's sister Ivy when staying with us liked to go over to Haldon House and help also. We enjoyed it because Pam was a bit of a comic, and we were always laughing at her. Pam found a little lamb where some animals would wander down the lane and get stuck in the brook.

Pam took the lamb back to the farmer, who said she could keep it if she thought she could rear it.

The lamb caused a lot of interest among the guests, who all wanted a go at giving it its bottle and having their photos taken with the lamb. Pam named it Lucy, who hung on to the teat very strongly which amused the guests; Lucy seemed to get through a large amount of milk.

This was all good fun until Lucy ate one hundred and fifty wallflowers that had been planted.
"She has got to go," said Ronnie, "she has now started on the roses."

So Pam took her back to the farmer, who paid her eight pounds for her. They all used to go over the farm to see Lucy, she had had her tail docked so all the lambs looked alike, but Lucy knew her name and came running. The farmer complained she thinks she is a dog she is always sitting on my doorstep.

When Angela was two her Dad and Mum bought her a Welsh Mountain Pony. Her love for horses started from that day. My sister Rose and her husband Jeff were staying at that time, and they never forget the picture that tiny blonde made when they sat her on that pony.

Pamela was carrying again and was expecting any time now and when it happened, there was another lovely little girl to fuss over. She was such a good baby, no trouble at all. Angela loved her little sister, she had a playmate at last; they called this beautiful little girl Elaine.

The new baby Elaine was a loveable child and had a cheeky grin, which made her adorable.

When the children were a little older, and when they were put to bed, I told them stories and got them to sleep, but Grandad was the favourite. When we took them out in the car, they loved to hear Grandad's songs, e.g., 'The Cat Flew Up The Chimney', or 'When The Old Dun Cow Caught Fire'. I said to him should they be singing 'booze booze booze the fireman cried, when the old dun cow caught fire'? But I was voted down, so as they seemed very happy, I joined in. We used to take them up on the racecourse, sit on the grass verge with our lunch and watch the racing when there was any on. Happy days.

It was a shock to Ron that the previous owner wasn't paying the right amount of rates, they had trebled, and it would happen to him in the winter months. Live and learn. Winter brought a couple of feet of snow that year, so we stayed and didn't try to get home to Teignmouth; it was a snowman and snowball Christmas – the children loved it. We couldn't open the door there was so much snow against it, but that did not stop us: we climbed out of a window.

Pamela's third baby was another girl. After waiting six years for a baby, Pam had her three girls in four years. Angela and Elaine wanted their new sister named Dawn, so Dawn she was; Pam said her family was complete, and she was happy with her three little girls.

Angela was going to the village school, and Pam was to put Elaine's name down now, even though it would be two years before she went.

Visitors always wanted to see the children, to take pictures of them, or to take them out, as they were well behaved. When the Rose Llalam Conference came to stay we helped as usual. They came from many different places, Switzerland, and the like; they went around the house to see if they could feel any vibes – they were touching walls and mantelpieces. One person would say, "This room has seen a lot of unhappiness a long time ago", another said, "There was a girl lying on this floor in soaking wet clothes, as if she had been pulled out of the river, a long time ago".

It made me feel all goose pimply; I did not stay around any longer – I made off.

There was only one corner of Haldon House left.

The two brothers who owned it were supposed to have gambled it all away. The lead from the roof, the lovely gilt mirrors from the ballroom, all of it. Some information may be gleaned from Mr Archie Winkworth who lives at Dunchideok House not far from Haldon House, or from the two old gentlemen who live in the Belvedere Tower.

They have a bust of General Lawrence there, and something about the Kohinoor Diamond, and old books on Telegraph Hill, from where the first telegraph was sent.

I would have loved to have found out more about the history, of all the fascinating history of Devon, but we were busy helping Pam and Ron. Bert used to do a lot of washing up and I minded the children, and helped when I could. There was a Lord Palk who owned the house and all of Haldon. But that is another story.

The original owner, Lord Palk of Haldon, owned all of Haldon, right down to Haldon pier in Torquay; it was when he died that his two sons gambled most of it away. Looking from the front of the building, there was a big Adams Archway. You walked through into the courtyard, and on the right there were three large stable doors, and this side of the courtyard was piled high with soil and rubble. Ron and Pam decided to clear it – the rubbish was there before they took it over. We all got to work on it. Bert took charge of the wheelbarrows. When they were full he ferried them down the lane to where there was a place that needed filling.

To Ron and Pam's delight they got down to the original cobbles. They hosed and cleaned them, and could hardly wait to plant trees and shrubs round the sides.

When the courtyard was all planted it was no time at all before they looked as if they had always been there. Ron said, "We will christen it with a barbecue." We all shouted yes. The children had never had a barbecue, but they were soon to find out what they were like. Bert and myself usually went to Rose and Jeff's in May; when we went to Devon they moved to Weeley, near Clacton, so we were off to Weeley for our usual visit.

When we returned Ron said they would like to spend a week in Spain, if it could be managed, before they got busy. Ron contacted his Mum and Dad and they said yes, they would be pleased to come down and take over the children. Ron only took seven guests for that week, and said he had booked a beach hut for the week, to take the children to. Ron's Mum was lovely with the children. Dawn was only about one and a half. She washed and dressed the three children while I got breakfast, then I packed them lunches and off they went to the beach hut in Teignmouth.

Well, our guests were very good, they got into the spirit of things, made their own beds, and cleared the tables while I got on with the vegetables for dinner. Bert did all the washing up, he was known as the gentleman with the pink hands. So things ran smoothly. We were able to join the others on the beach, and left the beach early, in plenty of time to cook dinner, saying, "See you later; be nice and hungry".

They said, "We will."

Pam and Ron looked well when they came home, so did we all, it had been a good week all round weather-wise. As luck would have it, Ron's Mum and Dad said they had enjoyed their meals and the guests seconded that; Pam and Ron said they felt fighting fit, and felt very refreshed. I was glad to hear it: they needed the rest, with Easter just gone, a busy time.

Angela, Elaine and Dawn were very good, but then they always were.

Peter started working privately and got lots of work; the gas company also gave him some jobs.

Diana's Dad, Bill, came down from Essex to work with Peter to help get him started, and stayed a couple of months. Peter worked at this for a few years but got tired of people keeping him waiting for his money.

He got taken on by North Sea Gas, as a foreman; his office was in a big van, wherever the men were working.

When North Sea Gas was finished, he went to a housing site being built along the river Exe, and was taken on as foreman gas fitter and plumber, and worked there until the site was nearly finished. He said to Di, "I must start looking for my next job, as the site is nearly finished."

One day Di was looking through the paper and she said to Pete, "There's a job going at Exeter University, why don't you put in for it? They are looking for a foreman."

Peter said, "A lot will be going for it."

"You have the qualifications," said Di, so he went and put his name forward. There must have been about a hundred there for it.

Peter was asked to go back to the university where they told him he had been shortlisted to six.

When he told us on the phone, we said we would keep our fingers crossed. The next we heard, he had got the job.

Pete had two girls, Jane and Lisa, they were about the same ages as his sister Pam's girls.

At this time they were still in the house in Stoke Cannon but were thinking of getting a larger house. This they did, near Honiton, in a pretty little village called Talaton.

It had four bedrooms, two toilets, a bathroom and shower, a lounge, dining room, long garden and garage, and the view was lovely.

Peter liked diving, football and squash. He got on well with people; his Dad was very proud of him. He had done well at his work, and I am glad his Dad made him stick at his apprenticeship.

After twenty-three years and two children, his wife left him for another man. Pete said, "I can do nothing, she loves this other man."

I found it hard to forgive at first, because Bert was so hurt. He would wake up in the night, and ask me why. I tried to comfort him but in the end I had to say please don't wake me Bert, you know how hard it is for me to get to sleep. This situation happens to such a lot of people, and some are your friends, that you get hardened to it after a while.

Peter had heaps of friends. Talaton is such a friendly village. His daughter Lisa is a nurse, and has a nice little home of her own.

When our friend Eddy had his band, one of his players was named Ron Purver. He was a smashing cornet player or very good on any instrument. Eddy always played the piano. When Eddy gave up the band then Ron Purver took over, and they called themselves, 'The Teign Valley Stompers'. As Ron lived in Teignmouth and Eddy and

Ivy moved to Southend on Sea we used to go and see the band a lot, and it was always a really enjoyable evening.

They are sometimes at The London Hotel in Teignmouth. We have been to the Coaching House Inn in Chudleigh to see them. We went to the Golden Butterfly, Torquay once to see them, as well; I love to hear them play the old tunes, like in a Persian Market, as it was played years ago. Great stuff.

Eddy plays for the blind in Southend on Sunday afternoons, voluntarily, and they love it with all the old songs and have a lovely singalong.

When Pam and Ron came home from Spain, they said they had been talking about giving up Haldon House. Pam wanted a little house, where she could have her three little girls round her.

Pam wanted what she called a normal life, with her children at school nearby. Ron said they would give it a little more thought.

Things went on the same for a while with guests coming and going. One day there was a storm and Rebel the dog made off in fright. Bert and I went out looking for him. Someone said he had been seen in Chudleigh, so every day we headed in that direction, without much luck. Pam asked a farmer if he had seen him, and the farmer said no, but if I do I shall shoot him as we are lambing here. Pam said, don't do that, he has been brought up with lambs. She was so worried that she even dreamed about Rebel. Her dream was so real. Pam said she could see this little old couple outside their cottage talking to the dog.

We were all nearly giving up hope of ever seeing him again when Pam said she would go and see if she could find this little place that had been in her dream. I shall know it if there is such a place, she said, and off she went back to Chudleigh to look. Pamela found what looked like the place, so decided to leave the car there with his rug and a dish of food in the open boot.

The next morning they went to see if they had been successful, and there was Rebel lying in front of the car. You would have had to run him over if you tried to move the car. Good thinking by Rebel: he had been missing seven days. He was in a very sorry state, but we were all happy to have him back with us. Another time some guests took Dawn up to the television room with them where there were big windows and a wide cushioned window seat. Dawn climbed on to the window seat, and the window was slightly open so out she went. Pamela rushed out and took her to Exeter Hospital. She had a large bump on her head so they kept her in overnight and fetched her home the next day. She was OK except for the bump, though we had all had a fright.

Well, if anything made them more determined to move it was that.

One more event was to happen before they actually moved out. Pam and Ron were closing and were going to have a few days at Ron's Mum and Dad's, but four guests begged to let them stay, saying they would look after themselves.

One of the dogs was going to their friends' kennels, and the guests would feed Fable. Ron said there is plenty of food for Fable, so this they agreed to do.

But there was a mix up and instead of taking Rebel, they took Fable – the dogs looked exactly alike.

Poor Fable: she missed her son Rebel, she missed the children.

The people at the kennels phoned Pam and Ron, and Pamela phoned me. I had friends to dinner at the time, but I just sat and wept. Ron had a post mortem done on Fable, and was told that she had died of a broken heart.

We were all very upset, because we all loved her and hated to think of what she had gone through.

Moving was definite now. The house was up for sale and several people came to look over it.

Pam and Ron had loved their time there, although it had been hard work at times, and they had ploughed a lot of money back into it. They had been there nearly ten years. They were now looking forward to getting a place in Ide, a pretty little village about two miles away. Bert said he was glad they had made the decision to move: "It will be better for the children, and to be nearer to school perhaps, and Exeter will be quite near too. It will be a different lifestyle, I quite like the idea."

Bert smiled and looked at his hands – he quite liked being the gentleman with the pink hands – and chatting to different guests was very interesting at times.

Bert went with Pamela into Ide, only a couple of miles away. They were looking at vacant property. Ron stayed behind, as they were expecting someone to view the house. Some of the places they looked at were unsuitable, but there was a little cottage, only a two up and two down Bert said, a bit small. Pamela said, "Yes Dad, but an acre of ground for the pony." Bert said, "Yes, there is that."

That afternoon we all went to look. That is, Pam and Ron, Bert and myself, and Dawn – the other two girls were at school. We would pick them up later.

There was an old lady in the cottage. She was blind, but she let us in, and asked us to sit down.

There was a toilet and bathroom, and a lounge, and the kitchen we were sit sitting in, downstairs. Upstairs were two bedrooms.

After a lot of discussion, Ron and Pam decided to take it. For now Ron said, the three girls can have the larger bedroom and we can manage in the smaller one.

On going back to the agent, they found they had been gazumped for another six hundred pounds. That happened a lot in those days. They had not seen anything else suitable so they took it. Ron had interviewed four people that week, all interested in Haldon House. The people that actually bought it had sold their own house for a goodly sum. Ron should have charged more for it but was eager to start his new life.

One good thing, they loved Ide.

Ron was looking round for some work. Jobs were never easy to come by, but he said he would take anything that came along. He found a place that let out farm machinery and they took him on. He had to deliver the machines to the hirers, and pick them up when they had finished with it.

He was also keeping his eyes open for something better.

One day he saw in the paper a firm that was looking for people to pump foam into walls. Pam said, "Try it Ron."

So Ron did and a smart looking lorry was delivered with the foam. A man was with it to get him started, he showed Ron how it was done, and he took to it like a duck to water – when people said they were pleased with the job, he said they could say so to the firm.

Ron could do three or four houses a week, so he could have the rest of the week off. He liked the work, and it was good money; sometimes Bert went with him.

That work came to an end when the cowboys got in and spoilt it. Some people thought that filling up damp walls would cure the damp, but these walls should not have been filled; people should have had them dried out first.

That meant Ron was once again looking for work.

Someone told him that the prisons were looking for warders so he told Pam that he would go and see. They told him that he would have to do three months' training. He agreed, and went to Wakefield to train.

Pamela told the children that Daddy had to go away to learn about his new job. Angela the eldest, said, "How long for Dad?" Ron said,

"Three months dear, not long." Elaine and Dawn wanted to know if that was a week. Ron said, no a bit longer than that. Angela went to say something and Ron stopped her. Ron said if it is possible to get home for some weekends, I will. After saying good-bye to his family, he was off. As it happened, some of the other fellows also wanted to try and get home, so after a couple of weeks, they managed to hire a car. They did not come every weekend as it was costly even with four sharing.

When the three months were up, they got a few days off before starting work. The work was varied – sometimes it was duty on the gate, or accompanying prisoners to the assizes, or to other prisons. It surprised me that they sometimes went by taxi. At that time there was plenty of overtime, as prisons were short handed, so Ron worked most weekends.

One day Pamela found a baby pig lying in the brook. It had wandered down the lane from a farm nearby and had fallen into the brook. Pam rescued it, but the side of its face that had been in the water was disfigured. She quickly wrapped it up and took it to the farmer, who said that she could keep it. Luckily Pam owned a little pigsty down by the gate where she laid the baby pig on some straw.

We always took him titbits. He was a friendly little chap, always standing on his back legs looking over the wall to see who was going by.

He grew very big, and when they could keep him no longer they took him back to the farmer who said, "What a long pig. There's a lot of rashers on his back."

Pam said, "Please don't say that."

"It must have been all that stretching up the wall," the farmer said, and paid fifteen pounds for him.

We all sadly dwelled on Twiggy's fate and it made us remember Haldon House and Lucy the lamb.

Meantime the house was growing. The lounge was made twice as big, with the other end a dining room, a modern kitchen and a utility room, and over the top were now four bedrooms, a bath and shower, and a toilet; downstairs was another toilet, bidet, and washbasin.

Their last big expenditure was a big round conservatory where we all liked to sit and enjoy the garden. Their dogs now were a bulldog and a bull terrier and they had two stables where they were sometimes put; they also had two double garages built: a lot of money had been spent. Although we had a lovely view ourselves, we loved to go and look at Pam's views.

The children were the biggest draw for us, and Peter and his daughters Jane and Lisa often came over. It was nice to all be together.

Pamela kept the children well occupied: they did gymnastics, sports, acro, ballet, and they liked doing it.

Pamela and a friend, Doreen, put on shows in Exeter which were well supported, and they were always being asked to put on more shows. They did a lot for charity, – we loved going to see them.

They once put on a comic skit, and Peter fell off his seat laughing. Pamela was a good choreographer; I thought she had talent – she had everyone laughing.

Angela and her partner Anna came second in Great Britain for Sports Acro, and had to travel to Coventry to try and win the Gold, that was in March 1979. They were Silver medalists and were seen on TV. They did not win Gold but retained the Silver, and a lot of people said they should have won, including some Coventry people.

That was Sports Acro for under thirteen year-olds.

We gave them a good homecoming, they deserved it.

As they grew older and Angela's partner grew taller than Angela, they let it fizzle out and did other things, and the perfect time is somehow lost.

Pamela was also a judge at competitions, and was sometimes called upon to judge.

All the girls at the club gave their time putting on shows in parks or in shopping centres in the summer to entertain the public. Angela took her pony to give rides for charity, and collected quite a bit, all for a good cause.

Silver was a white Welsh Mountain pony. She has had her horse called Penny for a number of years now.

Penny has had two lovely foals, the present one is nearly a year old now and is beautiful.

Angela rents a couple of stables over at Woodbury Common, and no matter what the time is when she finishes work, she sees to her horses first before returning home; she is really dedicated to them.

Our last car was a white Mini, and we were forever spending money on it. We liked the Mini because it was nifty and easy to park. Peter said to his Dad, "Why not sell it – you don't really need a car. We have two cars, and Ron and Pam have two – you have only to phone and we will take you where you want to go", so we settled for this.

Peter's daughter Lisa wanted to get a job as a nurse in Sheffield mainly because her boyfriend was at university in Sheffield, so this she did.

Jane, Peter's eldest girl, was working at the NicholCentre in Exeter, and is now working at Macdonalds, and Greenslades; she is a hard working girl, and very generous as with most girls like herself: she is slightly retarded, but likes writing letters, and the average person would not know that anything was the matter. She can do most things.

When they were having Jane, their first baby, there were so many babies being born in Exeter at the time that anyone with the facilities had to have their baby at home. Well, Peter's house was considered suitable. I don't think anyone having their first child should have it at home. Di was only tiny, and she was three days in labour; the Doctor was late, and it was left to the midwife to bring Jane into the world, otherwise I think things would have been different. Still, I suppose it's all water under the bridge now. Lisa has just bought her own little house in Sheffield.

She was explaining it to me one weekend, when she was here on leave – it sounds lovely, I should love to see it.

Lisa moved in about a month ago, and is happily settled in. She is now a fully fledged nurse, and when the babies' hospital in Sheffield was on TV a short while ago I did not see Lisa, but as the camera was going through a ward door, I saw her name at the top of a list – it said: 'In Charge, Lisa Morgan', and that gave me a thrill.

Lisa told me she is working sometimes over her time, and no one comes to relieve her, and they do not pay her any overtime.

I said they should not be allowed to get away with it.

We know the hospitals are short-staffed, but it is hard on the nursing staff. Lisa says so many babies are dying, and she gets asked to lots of funerals, it is very traumatic.

Let's hope that they all soon get the wages they deserve.

Frank Farrant was given a big party for his fiftieth birthday. Frank is my sister Rose's second son. The lovely thing about this party was that it was the coming together of parts of the family that we had not seen for many years.

For instance, my brother Richie's family, Stella and Gwen and their partners John and Bill, and although their brother Frank could not come, his daughter Deborah could: a lovely girl we had never met before.

Also the arrival of Ron Amato and his wife Pearl was another pleasant surprise. Ron was my Uncle Terry's son, whom we had not seen for years. The party was held in the Moose Hall in Shenfield – needless to say, we enjoyed it immensely.

After the dancing, while we sat and rested, a film show was put on, a sort of 'This Is Your Life' which showed Frank as a baby. He looked like a pixie in his pointed hat, and was shown at various stages in his life playing rugby, football, and swimming, up until the time he and a friend built his swimming pool. All they antics they got up to: there was a lot of laughter.

The supper was lovely, and as well as the lovely spread there were large bowls of jellied eels. I had not seen jellied eels for years – it's not something that you go in for in Devon. It was a wonderful party, and we intended to keep in touch with all our long lost relatives.

The next time we were all together was at my sister Rose's eightieth birthday party held in Braintree, where another lovely time was had. Rose looked lovely, although she was in a wheelchair, and my sister-in-law Nell was there. She is in her nineties and still going strong. I had a little dance with her. It was through Nell's efforts that our relatives were traced: she is the matriarch of our family.

Pam's Ronnie had been working in Exeter Prison a few years now. He never spoke about his work – they had to maintain a silence about what went on in prison. But if he got hurt at any time, then he told us how it happened. Usually I heard through Bert.

Bert told me that Ron had been watching these two men that had been pumping rather a lot of iron. Bert explained that meant they had been lifting weights, and exercising a lot. Well, one day, they trapped Ron, when he was on his own, and set about him. Ron was ready for them, he knocked one chap out, but the other one had got him round the neck, and was banging Ron's neck against the wall. Ron could not reach the alarm, but luckily another warder came running to his assistance and released Ron; other warders came on the scene and picked one up off the floor and put the men in their cells. Ron was given a couple of weeks off but he was back at work in three days: he had some bruised knuckles, and a grazed forehead. Ronnie is not a big beefy warder, like most. He is slim and incredibly strong, the prisoners didn't know this, but if they had seen him toning up in the gym, they would have known that he could lift weights a lot heavier than they could manage. I never liked Ron working as a warder – I used to say to Pam that he might as well be in prison himself.

Pamela at this time was working in Barclays Bank, part-time. Pam had been working full time, but wanted to go part-time and got her wish, and then she was able to do other things that she otherwise could not have done.

Glad to say she was able to see us more often.

Angela had been sitting her exams. She got one A- and nine O-Levels. When Pete's daughter came to see us, Lisa, who is two years younger than Angela, she said, "Angela's marks are academic, she should not be selling cigarettes in the booth in Tesco, she should have a far better job than that." I said, "I think she is only filling in for some pocket money." I was right: today they are both nurses, one in Sheffield and one in Exeter. Pam and Peter are justly proud of them. Pam's middle daughter, Elaine, has a good job on the council and Dawn also, on births and deaths on the computer.

When Dawn, Pam's youngest girl, first worked on computers, she did not find it easy: the strain on her eyes gave her many headaches. We told her if she could overcome this and stick at it she would have a good job in the end, which I am glad to say she did.

Elaine's job was just as hard, dealing with people having to pay their Poll Tax, people who were moaning and grumbling about it, with them saying, "Its all right for you, you have a good job." Elaine would say, "Yes, but I have to pay my Poll tax." On looking out of the window, she would see these grumblers getting into good cars. Others would want her to listen to their life story. It was a bit traumatic at times but, glad to say, she stuck at it, and it is a very good job.

Ron was to be in another scrap in his job. One day this big fellow broke out of his cell. Ron chased him and caught hold of him, and brought him down. Another warder came running. At this time Ron was kneeling, holding onto the prisoner, but his right foot was twisted under his other leg. Thinking nothing of it until his ankle began to swell, he ended up having difficulty walking and had to have time off. When his foot was X-rayed he had twisted a ligament, and as it did not improve they decided to operate. The operation did not make much difference; he was off work for a long time.

It was decided another operation would probably make him limp. Ron was to be on sick pay for nearly two years. At the end of that time the Prison Service retired him. Ron was of course glad that they had come to a decision at last: he was fifty-six years old.

Pamela was glad about this as she was hoping to retire at Christmas. Her boss at Barclays Bank said to her, "Pamela, would you like to retire the same time as your husband?"
"Yes, I would please." Pam could hardly wait to get home and tell Ron. She was also fifty-six years old.

When I saw them after this they were already planning a holiday.

Bert's sister Ivy came to stay as usual.

She loved Devon, she also loved Norfolk, and her home town. We had some good times. Pam used to come over and take us out. We often went over to Shaldon, a favourite place of ours. We liked to look at the river and the sea, and all the yachts; a colourful kaleidoscope, pleasing to the eye – we would spend hours there and never get tired of looking. Another favourite was Babbacombe: to sit on the green was very peaceful and there were plenty of places to eat there.

Or we would take some lunch up on Haldon Golf Course, where you could see all the coastline around for miles. We would take the binoculars with us to pick out all the places we knew. Bert was very good at spotting them, Bert also never forgot a face.

Another thing about Bert: he was in his element among people – friends and family – at gatherings like weddings and parties. He really showed an interest in their lives, and really liked to know how they were getting on. Everyone called him Uncle Bert, so consequently everyone liked talking to him: he was everyone's uncle.

It was while Ivy was staying with us that Bert wasn't feeling very well. On Saturday evenings, when Ivy, I, and a neighbour next door but one went to the club to play bingo, Bert went to this neighbour's house to chat with her husband. When we came home, we used to ask the men, had they put the world to rights? Anyway, they had covered a lot of ground, laughing and saying, "To be continued next week".

The following Friday Bert was in a lot of pain, and kept saying he did not want the doctor, but he could not sit or lie down. It got so bad that at last he agreed to have the doctor, so I sent for him. It was nearly eleven by then. The doctor asked why we had not sent before. I had to tell him that Bert didn't want the doctor. He understood that some men are like that. The doctor put some little tablets under his tongue, and a little later said, "Do you feel a little easier, old chap?"

Bert said, "Yes thanks." He then said, "I will send the ambulance for you now, and examine you in the morning."

When the ambulance came, two nice men said, "He will be all right with us." I made to go with him, but they said they would look after him. It was nearly twelve, so I said to Bert that I would be there very early in the morning, with his newspapers, spectacles, and his clean pyjamas. We watched him go, saying to Ivy there is nothing we could do, so we went to bed. At ten to five the next morning, the phone rang. We both reached it together.

A voice said, "Is that Mrs Morgan?"
I said, "Yes, speaking."
"Well, I am sorry to tell you that your husband is very ill."

We were both very shocked: the voice said can you come at once. We went to scramble into our clothes when it rang again and the same voice said, "Mrs Morgan, I am sorry to tell you your husband has died."

I said to Ivy he must have been dead the first time she phoned, the voice said can you come as you are. I said I will phone my son and daughter and come with them. I phoned Peter and Ron who were both very shocked.

I made Ivy and myself a small brandy, and then we washed and dressed. Peter, Pam and Ron arrived, and we climbed into the car. No one spoke, we were all too shocked.

Ronnie took me aside at the hospital, and said, "Pam doesn't know."
I turned to Pete and said, "Can you tell her?"

Ron said, "I just could not." You can just imagine poor Pam.

The sister took us into a little room, and Bert was looking very peaceful. I knew he could not hear me but I just had to tell him how sorry I was not to be there with him. The sister said, "He did not die alone, I was there with him." I did not like to say that was not quite the same, but I thought it.

Peter and Ronnie made all the arrangements, and Ivy was staying another week and was a tower of strength.

Bert died on the twelfth of September 1987. He would have been eighty-seven years old on the sixteenth of November. We always said he was as old as the year. His sister, Ivy, died two years later, of leukaemia, and was buried in Norfolk. We all missed Auntie Ivy's visits.

Ivy's friends Maureen and Joe packed up all Ivy's photos and sent them to me. Looking through them I came across Aunt Polly and Uncle Jim, and I remembered some of the things that Ivy had told me about them. Auntie Polly was Bert's mum's sister. Ivy had told me that Polly and Jim worked for royalty in Windsor Castle: Polly worked in the house and Jim was a carpenter. He had done some beautiful carvings, and had also made a staircase. They retired with a good pension, and bought a house in or around Southend on Sea. This was long ago. I remember Aunt Polly and Uncle Jim were spoken of with a kind of reverence.

If I was to list all our friends that have died, it would read like an obituary column, that's the worst of out-living your friends and relatives.

When Pam and Ron retired this year, they went on a two and a half months' holiday. They sent cards from all over the place: New Zealand, Australia, Fiji, The Gold Coast, Cairns, DayDream Island; they had a lovely time. Peter went to Plymouth, diving. He looks bronzed.

Looking back over the years, I would never want another Christmas like the one in 1944, when the whole country was covered in snow – one of the coldest for many years. Coal was ice-bound in railway sidings; snow, fog and frost caused a temporary shortage.

There was a feeling of optimism, as our armies were in sight of the Rhine. Our Home Guard had been stood down, as the danger of a likely invasion had passed.

Some trains were illuminated, the first time for many years. Christmas puddings were made with whatever ingredients you could get; apples, carrots, prunes, and berries from the garden. Although we had a little extra meat ration, cheese remained at two ounces per person, also one egg a week each.

It was the New Year before our armies were able to advance towards Berlin.

Fifty years on, most of the people that took part in World War Two are history.

Times are not exactly Utopia as they should be for the elderly; most still have to struggle to live, except for the jumped-up few.

I think war veterans should be fêted and be able to enjoy what is left for them and theirs, instead of being second class citizens. Also the people who stood up to the bombing and the shortages: it will soon be too late for those that are left.

After five granddaughters, I have been blessed (Aug 1994) with a great grandson. You can imagine what a little boy in the family means. He is very welcome and we all love him and think he is the cat's whiskers.

My son and his family and my daughter and her family have been a source of great pride to me, and as I ponder my memories in the last chapters of my life, I feel Bert's presence very close.

He was born in 1900 – almost a hundred years gone in the blink of an eye – although it was only thirty years ago that Bert retired, in 1965, and we packed our belongings and left our little house in Sheppey Road, Dagenham, handing the keys in after thirty-four years (still getting our five shillings deposit back). We moved to Devon to be near our son and daughter.

I recall in such vivid clarity the picture of a van sitting outside our house in Dagenham, an enormous monster of a removal van. How it brightened up the rather drab winter rows of houses as the neighbours waved us away, with the great expanse of its sides printed like a giant mural.

Golden sun, blue sky, turquoise sea and yellow sand and a prominent palm tree in the foreground. The words, 'Come to sunny Devon – try a taste of Heaven', in an arch across the vista. And for us, it was.

I'm happy to say my dear Bert and I had twenty-one years together in our little bungalow situated on the side of a hill overlooking the mouth of the River Teign. We saw our grandchildren grow up and my home reverberates with the sound of children's laughter and happy memories.

Bert died on 12th September 1987. We used to walk along the esplanade and lean on the rails gazing out to sea, and watch the pilot boats coming in and out of the harbour after guiding the cargo ships safely through the narrow strip of deep water.

We'd watch the long flat red sand dredger barge suck up the sand and deposit it elsewhere, in order to keep the shipping lane open. A far cry from the troubled waters of Bert's youth.

Life has been good to us and growing old together was a pleasure. Now, in the year 1995, it is the fiftieth anniversary of D-Day and this has stirred many pictures in my rusty old memory.

It is fifty years ago since our armies reached and entered the concentration camps and the full horror of war became known to the rest of us.

At this moment in time, a peace agreement has been reached with a troubled Ireland off our own shores. A reason surely to be ever hopeful.

I pray for the future generations that they may have peace in their time.

Some of Bert's medals were:

1914-1918
Service medal colour silver with horse and rider, on the reverse side George V.

1914-1919
Gold colour, angel with wings spread, on reverse says 'Great War for Civilization'.

A silver medal with a picture of a warship, Divuturne Fidelis Sea, on reverse George VI, the last king.

1939-1945
Silver colour, lion standing over a serpent with two heads, reverse George VI.

The Atlantic Star, bronze colour.

The African Star, bronze colour.

1939-1945
Star, bronze colour.

Bert's ships in the First World War, as far as I can recall, were the:
HMS Glatton
HMS Cambrian
HMS Verity
HMS Aircraft Carrier Hermes
There were probably others during his twelve years signed on that I cannot recall.
Bert was called up two weeks before the Second World War and served on one ship, the HMS Arethusa, for the duration of his time at sea.

I think the future belongs to the young.

Let's hope they make a better job of it than the present custodians, although it looks as if there is a better chance of peace in the future than there has ever been.

They have my blessing.